PLANT BASED DIET FOR BEGINNERS

The Essential Cookbook to Lose Weight and Be Healthier

(Easy to Make, Delicious Vegetable Recipes for a Healthy Lifestyle)

John Applegate

Published by Sharon Lohan

© **John Applegate**

All Rights Reserved

Plant Based Diet for Beginners: The Essential Cookbook to Lose Weight and Be Healthier (Easy to Make, Delicious Vegetable Recipes for a Healthy Lifestyle)

ISBN 978-1-990334-05-4

All rights reserved. No part of this guide may be reproduced in any form without permission in writing from the publisher except in the case of brief quotations embodied in critical articles or reviews.

Legal & Disclaimer

The information contained in this book is not designed to replace or take the place of any form of medicine or professional medical advice. The information in this book has been provided for educational and entertainment purposes only.

The information contained in this book has been compiled from sources deemed reliable, and it is accurate to the best of the Author's knowledge; however, the Author cannot guarantee its accuracy and validity and cannot be held liable for any errors or omissions. Changes are periodically made to this book. You must consult your doctor or get professional medical advice before using any of the suggested remedies, techniques, or information in this book.

Table of contents

Part 1 1
Introduction 2
CHAPTER 1: HEALTH BENEFITS OF PLANT BASED FOOD 24
CHAPTER 2: OTHER BENEFITS OF HAVING PLANT-BASED MEALS 46
CHAPTEER 3: BURN FAT, LOSE WEIGHT AND GAIN ENERGY WITH PLANT BASED DIET 59
CHAPTER 4: HOW TO MAKE THE TRANSITION FROM AN ANIMAL-BASED DIET TO A PLANT-BASED DIET, ONE STEP AT A TIME 81
CHAPTER 5: RECEPIES OF PLANT BASED DIET 95
SMOOTHIE 95
Apple and fennel pomegranate smoothie 95
Cucumber, green apple and ginger smoothie 97
Carrots and tangerins smoothie 97
Avocado, spinach, banana and chia seeds smoothie 98
Apple and cinnamon smoothie 98
Pumpkin smoothie with oat flakes, cinnamon and star anise 99
Chocolate smoothie with chia and banana seeds 100
Blueberry smoothie with oat milk and banana 102
Peach smoothie with almond milk and fresh mint 102
Antioxidant smoothie with watermelon and grapes 103
Frozen smoothies with ginger and peanut butter 103
Apple, pear and cinnamon smoothie 104
Mimosa smoothie 106

Pineapple and fresh ginger smoothie ... 106
Soy, banana and peanut butter smoothie ... 107
Protein smoothie with oats, banana and barley ... 107
Persimmon and pear smoothie ... 108
Protein smoothie with almonds, banana and cocoa ... 109
Raw strawberry smoothie with hemp seed milk ... 110
Anti-cellulite smoothie ... 110
Mango Ginger-Cashew Smoothie ... 111
Creamy Zucchini Blueberry Smoothie ... 111
Blueberry banana almond butter smoothie ... 112
Kiwi and avocado smoothie ... 113
Chocolate, banana and almond smoothie ... 113
VELOUTE & SOUP ... 115
Potato soup with Saffron ... 115
Cream of pumpkin and potato soup with mushrooms ... 116
Potato and avocado cream ... 117
Cream of asparagus soup with potato balls ... 118
Cream of carrot, ginger and spiced chickpeas ... 119
Cream of cauliflower and coconut milk ... 121
Cream of Romanesco broccoli ... 121
Part 2 ... 123
Introduction ... 124
Chapter 1: The Basics Of A Plant-Based Diet ... 126
Chapter 2: Breakfast Recipes ... 136
Chia Seed Smoothie ... 136
Mango Smoothie ... 136
Quinoa & Chocolate Bowl ... 137

Vegetable Hash	138
Walnut Porridge	139
Granola	139
Breakfast Cereal	140
Fruity Oatmeal	141
Pecan Pumpkin Spice Oatmeal	141
Carrot Cake Oatmeal with Cream Cheese Frosting	142
Chocolate Walnut Oatmeal	143
Breakfast Burrito Filling	144
Tofu Breakfast Custard and Potatoes	144
Apple and Sausage French Toast Casserole	145
Granola	146
Granola Oats	147
PB&J Oats	148
Choco-Coco Milk Shake	148
Nutty Choco Milk Shake	149
Gritty Choco Milk Shake	150
Creamy Choco Shake	150
Raspberry-Choco Shake	151
Strawberry-Choco Shake	151
Almond Choco Shake	152
Gritty and Nutty Shake	153
Raspberry and Greens Shake	154
Spiced Almond Shake	154
Cinnamon-Choco Coffee Milk Shake	155
Mocha Milk Shake	156
Coconut-Mocha Shake	156

Nutritiously Green Milk Shake 157
Strawberry-Spinach Shake 157
Lemon-Mint Creamy Green Smoothie 158
5-Lettuce Mix Green Shake 159
Basil and Pine Nuts Shake 159
Rosemary-Lemon Garden Greens Smoothie 160
Lemon-Cilantro Greens Shake 161
Blackberry-Chocolate Shake 161
Strawberry-Coconut Shake 162
Coconut-Melon Yogurt Shake 162
Berry Nutty Shake 163
Berry Overload Shake 164
Berry-Choco Goodness Shake 164
Lemony-Avocado Cilantro Shake 165
Strawberry-Chocolate Yogurt Shake 166
Blueberry and Greens Smoothie 166
Avocado and Greens Smoothie 167
Chapter 3.Soup Recipes 168
Cauliflower Soup 168
Greek Lentil Soup 169
Broccoli White Bean Soup 170
African Lentil Soup 171
Artichoke Bean Soup 172
Chinese Rice Soup 173
Black-eyed Pea Soup with Greens 174
Beanless Garden Soup 176
Black-eyed Pea Soup with Olive Pesto 177

Spinach Soup with Basil 178
Red Lentil Salsa Soup 179
Caldo Verde a la Mushrooms 180
Shiitake Mushroom Split Pea Soup 182
Velvety Vegetable Soup 183
Sweet Potato and Peanut Soup 184
Chapter 4.Stir-Fried, Grilled, & Hashed Vegetables .... **Error! Bookmark not defined.**
Crusty Grilled Corn .... **Error! Bookmark not defined.**
Conclusion 186

Part 1

Introduction

It is only until recently that more and more people are starting to embrace the plant-based diet lifestyle. As to what exactly has drawn millions of people into this lifestyle is debatable. However, there is growing evidence demonstrating that following a primarily plant-based diet lifestyle leads to better weight control and general health, free of many chronic diseases. This book will take you through the basics of this lifestyle, its benefits and why it works, as well as give ideas on how you can revamp your pantry and start whipping up delectable plant-based dishes. Whether you are new to this lifestyle or familiar with it, this book is definitely a treasure. Enjoy!

What Is A Plant-Based Diet?

A lot of people are doing it; a lot of people are talking about it, but there is still a lot of confusion about what a whole food plant-based diet really means. Because we break food into its macro-nutrients: carbohydrates, proteins, and fats; most of us get confused about how to eat. What if we could put back together those macro-nutrients again so that you can free your mind of confusion and stress? Simplicity is the key here. Whole foods are unprocessed foods that come from the earth. Now, we do eat some minimally processed foods on a whole foods plant-based diet such as whole bread, whole wheat pasta, tofu, non-dairy milk and some nuts and seed butter. All these are fine as long as they are minimally processed. So, here are the different categories: Whole grains Legumes (basically lentils and beans) Fruits and vegetables Nuts and seeds (including nut butter) Herbs and spices All the above-mentioned categories make up a whole foods plant-based diet. Where the fun comes in is in how you prepare them; how you season and cook them; and how you mix and match to give them great flavor and variety in your meals. There are chapters in this book dedicated to plant-based recipes which can give you an idea of what you can whip up real quick in your kitchen or those special meals you can prepare for the family. As long as you are eating foods like these on a regular basis, you can forget about carbohydrate, protein and fat forever.

Now, some people might say, "well, I cant eat soy" or "I dont like tofu" and soon. Well, the beauty of a whole food plant based diet is that if you dont like a certain food, like in this case, soy, then you dont have to consume it. It is not a necessary component in a whole food plant-based diet. You can have brown rice instead of oats, quinoa instead of wheat; Im sure you catch the drift now. It doesnt really matter. Just find something that suits you. Just because you have made the decision to adopt a plant-based diet lifestyle,doesnt mean that is a healthy diet. Plant-based diets have their fair share of junk and other unhealthy eats; case and point, regular consumption of veggie pizzas and non-dairy ice cream. Staying healthy requires you to eat healthy foods–even within a plant-based diet setting.

Why You Need to Cut Back On Processed and Animal-Based Products
Youve probably heard time and time again that processed food is bad for you."Avoid preservatives; avoid processed foods"; however, no one ever really gives you any real or solid information on why you should avoid them and why they are dangerous. So lets break it down so that you can fully understand why you should avoid these culprits.

They have huge addictive properties

As humans, we really have a strong tendency to be addicted to certain foods, but the fact is that its not entirely our fault. Practically all of the unhealthy eats we indulge in, from time to time, activate our brains dopamine neurotransmitter. This makes the brain feel "good" but only for a short period of time. This also creates an addiction tendency; that is why someone will always find themselves going back for another candy bar – even though they dont really need it. You can avoid all this by removing that stimulus altogether.

They are loaded sugar and high fructose corn syrup

Processed and animal-based products are loaded with sugars and high fructose corn syrup which have close to zero nutritional value. More and more studies are now proving what a lot of people suspected all along; that genetically modified foods cause gut inflammation which in turn makes it harder for the body to absorb essential nutrients. The downside of your body failing to properly absorb essential nutrients, from muscle loss and brain fog to fat gain, cannot be stressed enough.

They are loaded with refined carbohydrates

Processed foods and animal-based products are loaded with refined carbs. Yes, it is a fact that your body needs carbs to provide energy to run body functions. However, refining carbs eliminates the essential nutrients; in the way that refining whole grains eliminates the whole grain component. What you are left with after refining is whats referred to as "empty" carbs. These can have a negative impact on your metabolism by spiking your blood sugar and insulin levels.

They are loaded with artificial ingredients

When your body is consuming artificial ingredients, it treats them as a foreign object. They essentially become an invader. Your body isnt used to recognizing things like sucralose or these artificial sweeteners. So, your body does what it does best. It triggers an immune response which lowers your resistance making you vulnerable to diseases. The focus and energy spent by your body in protecting your immune system could otherwise be diverted elsewhere.

They contain components that cause a hyper reward sense in your body

What this means is that they contain components like monosodium glutamate (MSG), components of high fructose corn syrup and certain dyes that can actually carve addictive properties. They stimulate your body to get a reward out of it. MSG, for instance, is in a lot of pre-packaged pastries. What this does is that it stimulates your taste buds to enjoy the taste. It becomes psychological just by the way your brain communicates with your taste buds. This reward-based system makes your body want more and more of it putting you at a serious risk of caloric over-consumption.

What about animal protein? Often times the term "low quality" is thrown around to refer to plant proteins since they tend to have lower amounts of essential amino acids compared to animal protein. What most people do not realize is that more essential amino acids can be quite damaging to your health. So, lets quickly explain how.

Animal Protein Lacks Fiber

In their quest to load up on more animal protein most people end up displacing the plant protein that they already had. This is bad because unlike plant protein, animal protein often lacks in fiber, antioxidants, and phytonutrients. Fiber deficiency is quite common across different communities and societies in the world. In the USA, for instance, according to the Institute of Medicine, the average adult consumes just about 15 grams of fiber per day against the recommended 38 grams. Lack of adequate dietary fiber intake is associated with an increased risk of colon and breast cancers, as well as Crohns disease, heart disease, and constipation.

Animal protein causes a spike in IGF-1

IGF-1 is the hormone insulin-like growth factor-1. It stimulates cell division and growth, which may sound like a good thing but it also stimulates the growth of cancer cells. Higher blood levels of IGF-1 are thus associated with increased cancer risks, malignancy, and proliferation.

Animal Protein causes an increase in Phosphorus

Animal protein contains high levels of phosphorus. Our bodies normalize the high levels of phosphorus by secreting a hormone called fibroblast growth factor 23 (FGF23). This hormone has been found to be harmful to our blood vessels. FGF23 has also been found to cause irregular enlargement of cardiac muscles – a risk factor for heart failure and even death in extreme cases. Given all the issues, the "high quality" aspect of animal protein might be more appropriately described as "high risk" instead. Unlike caffeine, which you will experience withdrawal once you cut it off completely, processed foods can be cut off instantaneously. Perhaps the one thing that youll miss is the convenience of not having to prepare every meal from scratch.

Plant-Based Diet vs. Vegan

It is quite common for people to mistake a vegan diet for a plant-based diet or vice versa. Well, even though both diets share similarities, they are not exactly the same. So lets break it down real quick.

Vegan

A vegan diet is one that contains no animal-based products. This includes meat,dairy, eggs as well as animal-derived products or ingredients such as honey. Someone who describes themselves as a vegan carries over this perspective into their everyday life. What this means is that they do not use or promote the use of clothes, shoes, accessories, shampoo, and makeups that have been made using material that comes from animals. Examples here include wool, beeswax, leather, gelatin, silk, and lanolin.The motivation for people to lead a vegetarianism lifestyle often stems from a desire to make a stand and fight against animal mistreatment and poor ethical treatment of animals as well as to promote animal rights.

Plant Based Diet
A whole food plant based diet in the other hand shares a similarity with vegetarianism in the sense that it also does not promote dietary consumption of animal-based products. This includes dairy, meat, and eggs. Whats more is that,unlike the vegan diet, processed foods, white flour, oils and refined sugars are not part of the diet. The idea here is to make a diet out of minimally processed to unprocessed fruits, veggies, whole grains, nuts, seeds, and legumes. So, there will be NO Oreo cookies for you. Whole-food plant-based diet followers are often driven by the health benefits it brings. It is a diet that has very little to do with restricting calories or counting macros but mostly to do with preventing and reversing illnesses.

TRANSITION STRATEGIES

Transitioning to a plant-based diet doesnt have to be difficult. With a little planning, its easy to get all the nutrients you need from plant sources without relying on processed, refined foods—and without feeling like youre missing out on anything.

Start with small changes

For many, the transition to a plant-based diet is gradual. Observing a "meatless Monday" is a great way to start. Begin with one plant-based meal a day and then move on to two meals a day. Start eliminating the worst offenders from your diet, such as bacon and cheese, and have a fresh vegetable dish or two with every meal.

Eat your veggies

The additional fiber in a plant-based diet can be a shock to the system for those accustomed to unhealthy processed foods; large quantities of meat; and few, if any, fresh vegetables, fruits, and whole grains. A gradual increase in your fiber intake can be beneficial if youre prone to digestive disturbance. Start by eating a big, raw salad every day. Increase the amount of beans,legumes, fruits, and vegetables you eat, while decreasing or eliminating meat, dairy, and eggs.

Have a plan

If youre new to the plant-based lifestyle, youll want to do some meal planning. Planning your meals, and maybe doing a little cooking on your day off, can eliminate the urge to backslide into unhealthy eating. Youll be less likely to give in and order that sausage and pepperoni pizza if youve shopped for healthy ingredients or have a veggie casserole in the freezer ready to pop into the oven when youre hungry but dont have a lot of time.

Seek inspiration

Websites, magazines, blogs, cookbooks—inspiration is out there for those who seek it. Dont be afraid to try new things.The worst that can happen is you wont like a dish or meal.I find that the foods and techniques Ive come to love the most are those I resisted making because I thought I didnt have enough time, or I assumed I wouldnt like the end result. Try something new a few times a week, add the dishes you love to your repertoire, and forget the rest.

Go faux!

Miss the meat? A whole world of meat substitutes is out there, waiting for you to sample, from Tofurky to "veggie" pepperoni. I dont advocate eating these processed foods every day, but they do help satisfy cravings for familiar foods. And who doesnt want a little soy chorizo or a grilled veggie dog in their life once in a while?

Explore new frontiers

The plant-based diet is a great opportunity to boldly go where youve not gone before. Whether you visit an Indian vegetarian restaurant or gather your friends to create a Middle Eastern meze, youll find that many cuisines throughout the world rely on very little (or even no) meat, with vegetables and whole grains forming the bulk of the meal.The "peasant cuisine" of the Italian countryside my grandmother favored included vegetables grown in the garden, a salad at every meal, plenty of fresh bread, hearty soups, and stews spooned over hot and satisfying polenta. Youll find recipes throughout this guide that rely on that tradition as well as ones that explore cuisines you might not be familiar with. Be daring, and jump on in!

Move at your own pace

Finally, adopting a plant-based diet is all about the journey, and each of us experiences that journey differently. Open your mind and heart, and commit to seeking health and happiness through your diet.Challenges will present themselves—when youre traveling, when youre a guest in someone elses home, or when youre just plain tired and hungry and tempted by the familiar. When you fall,dust yourself off and start over.Any change for the better is a good thing. Give yourself a break, and do the best you can.

Filling Your Plant-Based Pantry

When stocking your plant-based pantry, focus on healthy, whole foods in their natural, unprocessed state. In addition, try some of the specialty foods and ingredients that can make cooking fun and tasty.

Vegetables

Choose a wide array of fresh and frozen vegetables like salad greens; leafy greens such as collards or kale; mushrooms; cruciferous vegetables such as cauliflower and cabbage; and aromatics like onions, carrots, and celery. Frozen vegetables can be a nutritious alternative to fresh, and in-season vegetables from a local farm are more economical and flavorful.I stock my freezer with broccoli, peas, greens, and corn from the farmers market.

Fruits

Fresh fruits such as bananas, berries, apples, and pears are great to eat as is or to use in baked dishes. Frozen fruits are fantastic in smoothies and pies, and you should always keep a stock of peeled, ripe bananas in the freezer for baking emergencies.

Beans and legumes

Choose a variety of dried and canned beans and legumes to provide an inexpensive, easy-to-cook protein source. I keep lentils, chickpeas, black beans, kidney beans, and cannellini beans in my pantry. Many recipes in this guide call for canned beans because thats what most busy cooks rely on to get dinner on the table. Dont be afraid to cook dry beans from scratch though—its easy and economical.

Grains

Keep a variety of grains and grain-like seeds on hand, such as brown rice, basmati rice, cornmeal, whole-wheat pastry flour, all-purpose flour, wholewheat and semolina pasta, rolled oats, barley, millet, farro, couscous, rice noodles, and quinoa. If you follow a gluten-free diet, almond flour, gluten-free flour mix, and oat flour are wonderful additions to your pantry.

Oils and vinegars

Start with a good extra-virgin olive oil and a neutral-flavored oil such as grape seed. Coconut oil is great in curries and baked goods. Nut oils add flavor to baked goods and salad dressings, and toasted sesame oil brings a smoky, nutty flavor. Refrigerate oils you dont use every day. Apple cider vinegar, red wine vinegar, and balsamic vinegar provide plenty of versatility. Rice vinegar is fabulous in Asian recipes, while umeboshi plum vinegar brings a unique salty, sour, pungent flavor to dishes.

Nuts and seeds

Stash raw almonds and cashews in the pantry for baking, making "cheese" fillings and nut milks, and plain old snacking. Walnuts and pecans make everything more delicious, especially when toasted. Chia and flaxseeds are essential to the plant-based baking pantry and can be added to salads, fruit dishes, breads, and oatmeal. Roasted, salted pumpkin seeds (pepitas) are nice, too. Store nuts and seeds in tightly sealed glass jars, and freeze seldom-used ingredients.

Soy products

No plant-based pantry is complete without tofu, tempeh, edamame, and miso. Tofu absorbs the flavor of what its cooked with, making it ideal in curries and stews. Tempeh, a fermented soy product, has an umami flavor and meaty texture perfect for grilling, sandwiches, and casseroles. Edamame are whole soybeans and are good in soups, stews, and salads in the same way youd use beans. Miso is an essential ingredient when building umami flavor.

Condiments

Stock a variety of homemade and store-bought condiments to add to recipes or enjoy on cooked foods. Ketchup, hot sauce, whole-grain Dijon mustard, and plant-based mayo are essentials.

Plant-Based Cooking Techniques

Plant-based cooking is easy once you master some basic techniques and equip yourself with helpful supplies: a 2-quart (2L) or more saucepan with a tight-fitting lid; a steamer basket; an assortment of mixing bowls; spoons and spatulas; some heavy, rimmed baking sheets; and a large, heavy sauté pan. A food processor is a nice extra that cuts down on prep time.

Steaming vegetables

Steaming is a simple way to cook vegetables with maximum flavor and nutrition retention. To steam, bring several inches of water to a boil in a saucepan fitted with a steamer basket over medium-high heat. Add the vegetables, cover with the lid, and cook until the vegetables are tender. The table given in this section lists steaming times for several vegetables.

Roasting vegetables

Roasting brings out deep flavors from root vegetables, brussels sprouts, asparagus, broccoli, and winter squash. To roast, preheat the oven to 400°F (200°C). Cut vegetables into uniform pieces, and place in a baking pan lined with parchment paper. Toss with just enough olive oil to coat; season with salt, black pepper, and dried herbs (if desired); and roast, stirring once or twice, until tender and caramelized.

Tender vegetables such as asparagus will roast to perfection in less than 10 minutes, while winter squash and potatoes need more time—up to 45 minutes. Try roasting broccoli, cauliflower, rutabaga, sweet potatoes, turnips, mushrooms, zucchini, small onions, and even green beans!

Blanching vegetables

When you want vegetables to remain crunchy and fresh and preserve their bright green color, or if youre preparing to freeze in-season produce, youll want to do some blanching. To blanch, bring a large pot of salted water to a boil over medium-high heat. Prepare an ice bath by filling a bowl with cold water and ice. Cut vegetables into uniform pieces, and drop in boiling water (see the table given in this section for recommended times). Using a slotted spoon, remove the vegetables from the hot water, transfer to the ice bath, and drain in a colander or on paper towels.

Sautéing vegetables

A quick sauté lets you cook vegetables with aromatics such as onions, garlic, and herbs for fresh, fantastic flavor. To sauté, heat a small amount of fat, such as olive oil, over medium-high heat in a heavy sauté pan. Add onions, and cook for 1 or 2 minutes, stir in garlic, and cook for 1 more minute. Add vegetables to the pan, and cook, stirring frequently, just until vegetables are tender.

Mushrooms, tender summer squash, broccoli, spinach, and peas are all excellent candidates for the sauté pan.

Cooking rice

With the exception of Arborio rice for risotto, rinse rice before cooking it. Measure the rice, place in a large bowl, cover with cold water, and swish around with your hands to release the rices starch and any soil. Drain and repeat three times. Place the rice in a pan with a tight-fitting lid, add water, and set over medium-high heat. Bring to a full, rolling boil, stir once, and cover.

Reduce heat to the lowest setting, and cook for the time noted on the rice package. Remove from heat and let stand, covered, for 5 to 10 minutes before fluffing with a fork and serving.

Cooking pasta

Cook pasta in several quarts of boiling water, seasoned with about 1 teaspoon salt. Pasta needs plenty of water, and plenty of space to expand while cooking, so use your largest pot. Bring water to a full, rolling boil over medium-high heat, add salt, add pasta, and cook according to the package directions. Pasta is best when cooked al dente, or "firm to the tooth." Drain pasta, and toss with sauce. Do not rinse pasta unless youll be chilling it, as for pasta salad, because the added starch in cooked pasta helps bind it with the sauce.

Choose the right pot. Be sure you use a pot thats large enough to allow the pasta to move around while it boils. Overcrowding yields gummy results.

Al dente pasta .For perfect pasta, boil it only until its al dente, or cooked but still slightly firm to the bite.

Cooking dried beans

When cooking dried beans and field peas, soak overnight in plenty of fresh water. Drain rinse, and place in a heavy pot with 2 inches (5cm) water to cover. Bring to a boil over high heat, reduce heat to a simmer, add 1 teaspoon salt, and cook for about 1 hour or until tender.

If youre cooking kidney beans, you need to take an extra step. Raw kidney beans contain a toxin called phytohameaggluttinin, which can only be removed by cooking at the boiling point for 10 minutes. After bringing the beans and water to a boil, cook for 10 minutes, skimming off the foam that rises to the top. Then cook as directed. This step, while only 10 extra minutes, is essential.

Storing cooked beans. You can refrigerate beans in their cooking liquid for up to 5 days or freeze for up to 3 months.

Cooking lentils

Lentils do not require a soak and cook very quickly—as little as 20 minutes for red lentils and a little longer for other varieties. I like to cook lentils with a little onion and garlic to preseason them for recipes. In a medium saucepan over medium-high heat, heat 1 tablespoon olive oil. Chop a small onion and a few cloves of garlic, add them to the saucepan, and sauté for 3 to 5 minutes. Add 1 pound (450g) lentils with water or broth to cover by 2 inches (5cm). Bring to a boil, reduce heat to medium-low, and cook, partially covered, until tender.

Divide into 2 cup portions plus cooking liquid, refrigerate for up to 5 days, or freeze for up to 3 months.

Perfect protein
Lentils are the perfect plant-based protein—nutritious, delicious, versatile, quick-cooking, and affordable.

Cooking with tofu

Tofu is endlessly versatile. Its neutral in flavor so it takes on the flavor of whatever its cooked with. Drain tofu before using it in recipes by placing the block on a cutting board thats wrapped in a clean kitchen towel. Set a heavy plate on top of tofu, and add a heavy can on top of that. Let tofu drain for 30 minutes, pat dry, and proceed with your recipe. Tofu can be sliced as for cutlets, cubed for stews and curries, crumbled for an eggless scramble, or blended into cake batters in place of eggs.

Cooking with tempeh

For best flavor and texture, marinate and/or steam tempeh. To steam, cut tempeh into strips or slices. Place it in a baking dish, cover with marinade or vegetable stock, cover tightly, and bake until tempeh is puffed up. This tenderizes and flavors your tempeh.

Cooking with seitan

Seitan is a seasoned loaf made from vital wheat gluten that can be used to simulate the texture and flavors of beef or chicken. Try it grilled or seared in a cast-iron pan for use in sandwiches.

Basic seitan

You can find seitan in the refrigerated section of most grocery stores, or you can pick up some vital wheat gluten and make your own!

YIELD 2 (1-Pound/450g) Loaves **SERVING** 1/6 loaf **PREP** 10 mins **COOK** 30 mins

INGREDIENTS

5 cups vegetable stock
2 small yellow onions
2 cloves garlic
1 TB. plus 1 tsp. reduced-sodium tamari
1 TB. apple cider vinegar
1 tsp. Bells seasoning blend
1 tsp. baking powder
1/2 tsp. sweet paprika
1 3/4 cups vital wheat gluten
1/4 cup chickpea flour
1/4 cup nutritional yeast
1/2 tsp. fine sea salt
1/2 tsp. freshly ground black pepper
1 bay leaf
2 small pieces dried porcini mushroom (optional)

In a food processor fitted with a metal blade, blend 1 1/2 cups vegetable stock; 1/2 small onion, roughly chopped; 1 garlic clove, roughly chopped; tamari; apple cider vinegar; Bells seasoning; baking powder; and sweet paprika until smooth.

In a medium bowl, whisk together vital wheat gluten, chickpea flour, nutritional yeast, sea salt, and black pepper. Pour in wet ingredients, and stir with a silicone spatula until liquid is incorporated and a rough dough is formed.

Cut dough into 2 equal pieces, and use your hands to quickly knead into logs.

In a medium bowl, whisk together vital wheat gluten, chickpea flour, nutritional yeast, sea salt, and black pepper. Pour in wet ingredients, and stir with a silicone spatula until liquid is incorporated and a rough dough is formed.

approximately 6 inches (15.25cm) long if the seitan will be served sliced, such as in roasts, cheese steaks, or gyros; or break seitan apart into rough chunks for stews or skewered items like satay. Set aside, and allow to rest for 5 minutes.

Meanwhile, chop remaining $1 1/2$ onions into rough wedges. Place in a large saucepan with a lid along with remaining $3 1/2$ cups vegetable stock, bay leaf, remaining 1 clove garlic, and porcini mushrooms (if using). Set over medium-high heat, bring to a boil, reduce heat to medium, and gently add seitan loaves. Cover and cook over the lowest heat for 45 minutes without lifting the lid.

Uncover, remove bay leaf, and cool completely in broth before storing. Seitan will keep in the refrigerator, stored in its cooking broth, for up to 3 days, or can be frozen for up to 3 months. Defrost completely in the refrigerator overnight before using.

Meal Plans

When creating meal plans, think about your time, tastes, and the nutritional value of the foods youre eating. Also do as much cooking and prep work ahead of time as you can—a little work on your day off makes the rest of your week easier. Chop onions, celery, and carrots ahead; place in zipper-lock plastic freezer bags or containers in 1 cup portions; and use straight from the freezer— no need to thaw. Make a batch of granola on the weekend, and store it in an airtight jar for easy grab-and-go snacks. Soups and stews are ideal to make ahead and refrigerate or freeze for later. Prepare pizza dough up to 2 days ahead and refrigerate. Make a double recipe of Vinaigrette, refrigerate for up to 5 days, shake, and pour over weekday salads. Whenever possible, double a soup or casserole recipe and freeze some in individual-or family-size portions. Soon youll have a freezer full of meals ready to defrost whenever youre crunched for time.

Pie pastry

This easy pie pastry comes together quickly in the food processor and yields a flaky, tender crust perfect for sweet or savory recipes.
YIELD 1 double crust for a deep-dish pie
SERVING about 1/8 pie
PREP 10 mins, plus 30 mins rest time
COOK none

INGREDIENTS
3 cups unbleached all-purpose flour
1 1/2 tsp. kosher salt
12 TB. Non-hydrogenated organic shortening, partially frozen, cut into small cubes
4 or 5 oz. (120 to 150ml) ice water

In a food processor fitted with a metal blade, pulse all-purpose flour and kosher salt several times to combine.

Add half of shortening cubes, pulse 5 or 6 times, and run the food processor for 5 seconds. Add remaining shortening, and pulse until shortening resembles small, pea-size pieces.

Transfer flour mixture to a large bowl. Pour a few tablespoons ice water over flour mixture, and quickly toss with a large kitchen fork to combine. Continue adding water and tossing until mixture just comes together and then use the heel of your hand to press dough against the sides of the bowl to form a moist, cohesive ball.

Separate dough into two equal pieces, wrap in plastic wrap, and use your hands to flatten each piece into a 5-inch (12.5cm) disc.

Refrigerate dough for 30 minutes, and proceed as directed in your recipe.

Nut milk

Once youve tasted homemade nut milk, youll never go back to the store-bought kind.

YIELD 4 cups
SERVING 1 cup
PREP 5 mins plus overnight soak time
COOK none

INGREDIENTS

1 cup raw almonds, hazelnuts, or cashews
4 cups filtered water
2 or 3 pitted Medjool dates
1 tsp. vanilla extract
1/2 tsp. ground cinnamon

Soak almonds in cold water overnight.

Discard water that the nuts soaked in, rinse nuts well, and drain.

In a high-speed blender, process nuts, filtered water, Medjool dates, vanilla extract, and cinnamon until smooth.
Using a nut milk bag, jelly bag, or clean stocking, strain solids from milk.
Refrigerate milk in a clean glass jar for up to 4 days. Shake well before using.

Fresh pasta dough

You can easily make your own eggless fresh pasta dough for long shapes such as hand-cut tagliatelle or fettuccine, or filled pasta such as ravioli. For added flavor and a pretty golden color, try saffron or tomato paste—or both. Use a pasta machine to roll the dough if you have one; a rolling pin also works. Try a straight pin without handles for this.

CHAPTER 1: HEALTH BENEFITS OF PLANT BASED FOOD

A plant based diet is that which is made up of mostly of food substances from plant sources. A diet consisting of predominantly plants and very little food substances of animal origin can also pass for a plant based diet. This diet pattern is quite different from the vegan diet – while the vegan is totally about plant substances alone; the whole plant based diet seeks to bring to the barest minimum intake of processed food, limit to the types and amount of animal based food substances we take. So we will see that the whole plant based diet is more of a life style than a feeding routine because it also cuts across your psyche.

Look around the ecosystem, you will understand that the natural producers are plants, they are the only organisms empowered molecular structures to help them produce food substances from natural elements in the atmosphere and sunlight; this is what is known as photosynthesis – the ability of plants to produce compound food substances by using carbon(IV)oxide and water in the atmosphere in the presence of sunlight to produce food. Think through that; the plants were created in the ecosystem to be the producers, but we as humans go on to feed on animals which feed from plants. Now do not get me wrong, but do you not think it is better to go straight to the producer to get what I want fresh, than getting it from someone that has gotten from the producer, used what I want and then give me in turn – more like I become a second class user; do you understand what I am saying?

Think about it this way, if the ecosystem has designed it such that we all get from the producers, dont you think that it will come with extra cost to leave a producer to feed from a fellow consumer – I am just thinking out loud! But I believe having an animal based diet comes with consequences. Consequences that you do not need astronomical science to see in our world today. Well, there is a place for indulging and craving for what we have been taught to eat by society, of course in school we have been taught that we are omnivores and that we can eat both plant based food substances and animals too; but I am here to preach to you to cut down on animal based food and take more of plant based food – it is better to get the nutrition you need from the producers themselves – to save you "costs".

My first assignment in this book is to convince you by telling you the health benefits of plant based diets; it is no news that many of us dig our graves with our forks and spoons – the knife with which we cut those sumptuous and spicy animal muscles somehow comes for our throats later on in life. A little girl said "Cholesterol caused diseases like heart diseases, atherosclerosis et cetera are animals coming for revenge after being killed and eaten in cold blood", that cracked me up but it permeated the very soul of me! Like that statement though simple and coming from a cute little girl, carries profound truth – science has also proven this thing over the years. Like; it is so true that if you need a college professor to bring it your way, then you might be dumb. If you expect me to use breakneck statistics to amaze you, then you do not have the right book (just go to world health organization records and have your mind blown) this book is to guide you through a transition. Thinking on the words that little girl said, would bring a certain reality to you so fast that your hairs would curl – like it is so simple you will need someones help to misunderstand the message.

So probably if I am able to show you what is in this transition for you would help you begin to adjust to make the switch, because I will assume you love yourself. Generally speaking, plant based meals apart from being fresh and having a way of preserving every nutrient in the meal, they are generally healthier than animal based foods and processed food substances. Also on a general note, plant based diets have been strongly associated with reduction of heart diseases, obesity and a myriad of diseases caused by oxidative stress – which ingestion of cholesterol from animal sources induce; this should lead you to give thought to these things. Let us get into looking at the details of the health benefits of a plant based diet shall we?

REDUCES THE RISK OF DISEASES THAT CAN BE CAUSED BY OXIDATIVE STRESS

I am going to take this slow so that you will understand exactly what we are talking about here. The body is created to function in its optimum level given certain conditions such as perfect anatomy (structures) perfect physiology (functions) and perfect biochemistry (metabolism) – any deviation from this state leads to an anomaly or pathology (sicknesses and diseases). Now the systems in the human body work together to maintain this balance and perfect condition to keep us functioning and living at our best – this activity of maintaining the balance in your system is called homeostasis.

Now pay attention, as you interact with the environment and ecosystem (of which eating is one of those interaction), your temperature changes, your hydration level changes et cetera; your body begins to adjust to adapt to it or begins to adjust to motivate you to take care of whatever changes it is that needs to be taken care of – this is a large part of homeostasis. Where you begin to shiver as you feel cold, that is your body trying at least to vibrate vigorously to generate some heat. Alright, we are not in a physiology class, but, I am trying to point out something to you, that as you interact with your environment, there are changes in your body and your body also begins to make adjustments to take care of those changes and bring you back to functioning at your best or at least close to it – now in situations when the body is unable to bring you back to that optimum state by itself, there is a problem and there will now be need for medicine or other chemical substances that can help.

Animal based foods contain free radicals, though they are not the only substances that contain free radicals. The next question would be what are free radicals? A free radical is a molecule, atom or ion that contains free electrons which make them highly reactive and can trigger a chemical reaction in a chemical system; therefore free radicals in animal diets can come into the body and by their highly reactive nature can trigger off a reaction (these reactions caused by free radicals are called oxidative reactions) that the body cannot control. Now do not be too scared yet; the human body has natural antioxidants (these are compounds that terminate the oxidative chain reactions triggered by free radicals) such as uric acid found in the human blood, glutathione, ubiqinol, ascorbic acid, lipoic acid, carotene et cetera.

Now in a situation where the level of free radicals in the body and oxidative reactions caused by them cannot be matched and balanced out by the bodys antioxidant, an "oxidative stress" ensues – now depending on the part of the body where this oxidative stress occurs it can lead to various diseases such as; cancer, heart diseases, cataract, arthrosclerosis, diabetes, rheumatoid arthritis, post-ischemic perfusion injury, myocardial infarction, chronic inflammations, stroke. Apart from these disease conditions listed, oxidative stress can have a toxic effect on neural cells, which can lead to Alzheimers disease, Parkinsons disease and multiple sclerosis to mention but a few.

Oxygen and oxygenation are necessary for cell life, respiration and phosphorylation, as long as the oxygen and the free radical species are in check by the antioxidants. So an absence of antioxidants which try to keep the balance, these free radicals can cause untold damage to the body! So it is a two way thing, it is either you deliberately reduce the intake of substances that contain free radicals or you increase the intake of antioxidants – which a whole plant based diet will avail you the two at the same time; more like killing two birds with one stone.

This is fact; the effects of oxidative stress as a result of free radicals can be devastating. But there is good news, there are myriads of plants that contain antioxidants and a few animal sources of the same – let us look at them briefly!

DARK CHOCOLATES

This is made from cocoa, and contains antioxidants known as flavonoids (for example anthocyanine and quercetine), in addition to the antioxidants it contains dark chocolates are rich in minerals. According to research carried out by scientists, dark chocolates contains above 15mmol per 0.1kg; this is even more than raspberries that has 2.3mmols in 0.1kg and blueberries that have about 9.3 mmols per 0.1kg. Of course the antioxidants in dark chocolates have been found to reduce the risk of heart diseases and other chronic inflammations. More so, dark chocolates and other products from cocoa, reduce diastolic blood pressure by about 2.5mmhg, therefore it is good for preventing hypertension (diastolic the figure normally recorded as the denominator) and it reduces systolic blood pressure by about 4.5mmhg (systolic is the figure normally recorded as the numerator).

PECANS

Pecans are nuts that are native to South American continent – especially Mexico. They contain a lot of healthy fat, mineral and antioxidants (polyphenols). According to scientific researches, pecans contain about 10.5mmol of antioxidants per 0.1kg; pecans really help in raising the blood antioxidants and at the same time give about 25% fall in oxidized blood in the human circulatory system. The downside is that pecans contain high fats and high calories, so it is best eaten with moderation.

BLUEBERRIES

Blueberries as we mentioned before contains antioxidants just a little lower than dark chocolates, they also have very low calorie content. It has been stated in various scientific studies that amongst the commonly eaten vegetables and fruits, blueberries contain the highest amount of antioxidants – being abundant in anthocyanins, ellagic acid and resveratrol. Generally as we age brain function begins to decline, but the antioxidants contained in berries helps slow down that decline in brain function. Additionally, evidence has shown that anthocyanin in blueberry drastically reduces the risk for heart diseases by lowering cholesterol levels and blood pressure.

STRAWBERRIES

Strawberries are really sweet and one of the most common sources of antioxidants on earth; they contain a good amount of ascorbic acid (vitamin C) and other antioxidants – the presence of anthocyanin in strawberries give them their red color, so the more anthocyanin a strawberry has the brighter red it is. Each 0.1kg of strawberry has about 5.2mmols of antioxidant. Just like in blueberries the anthocyanin in straw berries reduces the risk of heart diseases by control blood cholesterol levels.

ARTICHOKES

Artichokes a leafy vegetable found in North America are rich in minerals, vitamins and antioxidants – every 0.1kg of artichoke contains about 4.7mmols of antioxidants. This delicious and nutritious vegetable is very rich in an antioxidant known as chlorogenic acid – which from studies have been proven to reduce chronic inflammations, reduce the risk of cancer, type two diabetes and cardiac problems. It is important to note that the amount of antioxidant you get from your artichoke will depend o how you prepare it – when boiled, the antioxidant content rises about eight times, when steamed it increases to about 15 times, but when fried the antioxidant content reduces drastically; so you will call the shot on how much antioxidant you want from your artichoke by how you prepare it.

GOJI BERRIES

Goji berries are native to China; they have been a part of Chinese medicine for well over two thousand years. These dried fruits are rich in vitamins, minerals and antioxidants – scientific studies show that these berries contain about 4.3 mmols of antioxidants per 0.1kg. the aging process in the human body is predominantly as a result of oxidative stress, but Goji berries contain an antioxidant called Lycium barbarium which slows down aging of the skin, in addition to that it also reduces the risk of cancer and heart diseases. Studies have shown a daily intake of goji berries for about 3 months can raise the blood antioxidant level by fifty-seven percent.

RASPBERRIES

Raspberries are a good source of ascorbic acid, manganese and antioxidants- containing about 4mmols of antioxidants per 0.1kg. A research which was carried out using animal models and test tubes showed that raspberries killed over 90% of breast, stomach and colon cancers; in addition to that it also slows down the occurrence of heart diseases as a result of oxidative stress.

KALE

Kale is a leafy vegetable rich in calcium, retinol, ascorbic acids, vitamin K and antioxidants – every 0.1kg of kale contains about 2.7mmols of antioxidants, although the red variations of kale may contain at least twice as much antioxidants than their green counterpart of the same mass; owing to the fact that red kale contains anthocyanin that gives it its bright red color.

RED CABBAGE

Red cabbages which are also called purple cabbages are rich in retinol, ascorbic acids, minerals, vitamin K and antioxidants – containing about 2.2 mmols per 0.1kg of antioxidants. These red cabbages contain about 4 times more antioxidants than the regular green cabbages because of the presence of anthocyanin. The ascorbic acid contained in red cabbages improves the immune system and also makes the skin firm. The way red cabbage is prepared determines how much antioxidant it would have – when it is fried it actually has more antioxidants but when it is boiled or steamed the antioxidant content in it reduces.

BEANS

Beans are legumes that are rich in fiber and help in bowel movement. Beans are a good source of proteins and antioxidants – every 0.1kg of beans contains about 2.0mmols of antioxidants. A specific antioxidant contained in beans helps suppress inflammatory processes and reduces the risk of cancer, this antioxidant in beans is known as kaempferol. Studies show that cancers of the breast, kidney, lungs and bladder are suppressed by kaempferol.

BEETROOTS

Beetroots are roots of Beta Vulgaris vegetable, they are rich in potassium, fiber, iron, folate and antioxidants – it contains about 1.7 mmols of antioxidants per 0.1kg. an antioxidant called betaalin gives beetroots their reddish color and scientific studies have shown that it reduces the risk of colon and digestive tract cancers additionally it helps suppress chronic inflammatory disorders like osteoarthritis.

SPINACH

Spinach has low calorie content but is very rich in vitamins, minerals and antioxidants – every 0.1kg of spinach contains about 0.9mmols of antioxidant. Lutien and zeaxanthin are major antioxidants found in spinach. Lutein and zeaxanthin are also found in abundance in corn; they are responsible for protecting the eye from the damaging effect of ultra violet rays that can be dangerous to the cornea, lens and retina of the eye. These antioxidants help combat cataract, retinitis pigmentosa, age-related macular degeneration and other retinopathies.
Other plant based food substances that are rich in antioxidants are: grapes, Brazil nuts, collard greens, broccoli, sweet potatoes, carrots, whole grain bread, brown rice and corn tortillas et cetera.

BOOSTS THE GENERAL IMMUNE SYSTEM OF THE BODY

As you have heard microorganisms are ubiquitous – that is to say they are everywhere, in our air, water, skin, bodies, surfaces, soil (just go ahead and keep naming) but the reason why you have not fallen sick is because of your immune system; the bodys ability to fight off infections and diseases is as a result of the immune system. Once the immune system is compromised like in the case of individuals that have HIV/AIDS or people that use steroids carelessly, these organisms in our atmosphere which would have otherwise been harmless to them because of the defensive work of the immune system would now be able to cause harm. So when the immune system is compromised, we are in trouble – luckily there are plant based diets that boost our immune system without any side effects.

You see, we would allow these health benefits convince you to make the switch, do not think you are making a sacrifice, eating healthy does not cost – it pays. Let us look at plant food substances that can boost our immunity shall we?

SPINACH

Spinach contains a very high amount of folate, magnesium, iron, fiber, retinol and ascorbic acid; these nutrients are important for boosting the bodys immune system and are necessary for DNA repairs and cell division in the body. You can only get the best from spinach with very little or no cooking at all.

GREEN TEA

All kinds of tea, both green and black are rich in flavonoids and other awesome antioxidants; these boost the bodys immune system. More so contained in green tea are amino acids such as l-theanine which help in the production of T-cells, special forces in your immune system that fight germs and disease causing organisms. Remember of course that what HIV tries to destroy are the T-cells making the individual immune-compromised and unable to fight diseases, making the person open to invasion by opportunistic infections. These antioxidants in tea also are known to reduce the risk of heart diseases because contained in tea especially green tea are lipids which help for the production of high density lipoproteins or good cholesterol (they are referred to as good cholesterol because they transport cholesterol from the blood back to the liver for more metabolisms, while bad cholesterol or low density lipoproteins carry cholesterol from the from the blood to every part of the body depositing them also in the lumen of blood vessels and damages)

CITRUIS FRUITS

Citrus are fruits that are very rich in ascorbic acids, whenever people catch a flu, they begin to take oranges or other citrus, the reason is because citruses contain vitamin C which boosts the immune system – increasing the resistance of the skin and the mucous membranes. They are also thought to help boost the production of leukocytes (white blood cells) which are responsible for attacking and destroying invading microbes in the body. Now because our body does not produce nor store ascorbic acids we need to have them in our meals as often as we can. Examples of citruses are; oranges, tangerines, grapes, lemons, limes and clemintines.

RED PEPPER

For the records peppers contain twice as much ascorbic acid than citruses, so this really makes them very great immune system boosters. More so they have a great content of beta carotenes. Apart from the fact that it boosts your immune skin it gives you a good skin texture, and improves your eye health.

BROCCOLI
Broccolis are packed with numerous vitamins and minerals and serve as good immune system boosters, it contains good amount of vitamin C, vitamins B1, B2, B3 and B6; and within the broccoli is the bodys chief antioxidant "glutathione" – it is best served without cooking, but if it must be cooked; cook it as little as possible.

GARLIC
Garlic has been one of the oldest "medicines" for curbing infection. It is one of the commonest spices found in the world. It has great allicine contents and other high sulfur containing compounds; they help lower blood pressure, prevent atherosclerosis, and boost the immune system. It has antibacterial, antifungal and antiviral abilities – the antioxidant contained in garlic can reduce the progression of Alzheimers disease, cancer and cold (fever). People that eat garlic have 30% less probability to have colorectal, liver and pancreatic cancer.

YOGURTS

Yogurts! Yeah, this a bit out of the plant box right? Yeah remember the intention here is not to make you vegan as it were, but to help you eat predominantly plant food and as little animal food as possible with zero tolerance for processed food. For yogurts, get one that has attenuated culture, not one whose culture is completely dead; you will see this indicated on the label. These cultures will help exercise your immune system and stimulate them to fight diseases. Plain yogurts are actually better than the sugary already flavored ones – you can easily add flavor to your plain yogurt by adding honey or other fruits as you please. Yogurts are also a good source of vitamin D – this regulates your immune system and improves your bosys ability to fight off diseases. In addition to this, they are also a good source of vitamins B2 and B12. Yogurts contain a lot of "probiotics" especially *Lactobacillus acidophilus, Lactobacillus casei,* and *Bifidus;* these probiotics are especially very good in dealing with cold and are also important for proper digestion and bowel movement.

TUMERIC

What most people know about turmeric is that it is a bright yellow spice used as curries or it can be used for facial or skin treatment, but further from that, turmeric has been studied and it is shown to contain a large amount of cur cumin – which is the reason for its color, it can heal muscle tears and wears, osteoarthritis and rheumatoid arthritis.

PAW PAW

Paw paw is a fruit that is rich in vitamin C, potassium and folate, which of course boosts the immune system. In addition to it, it contains an enzyme known as papain which mediates digestion and it has strong anti-inflammatory effects.

KIWI

Just like paw paw fruit, kiwis are rich in folate, potassium, vitamin K and vitamin C and we have seen over and again that vitamin C boosts the production of white blood cells and hence the overall immune system of the body.

SWEET POTATOES

Sweet potatoes are packed with an enormous amount of vitamin A (retinol) and vitamin C (ascorbic acids) with just little extra calories. These vitamins improve our skin appearance; they are good for the retina and also boost the overall functioning of the immune system. And you know what? There is no need to feel guilty munching on them sweet potatoes, they are totally free of fats and cholesterol; do not fear for your weight – they offer all this goodness and taste and adds no fat to you, good news right? And you know an additional part of sweet potatoes? They are rich in fiber! Sweet potatoes are just tubers of goodness!

HELPS REDUCE THE RISK OF HEART DISEASES

I want you to take not of this very important fact, and maybe say it out loud – Cholesterol is never found in plant based food substances, it can only be found in animal based food substances. You are going to know the significance of this statement as we move ahead.

Cholesterol is a shiny and waxy substances found in the blood; cholesterol is important for the formation of healthy cells, especially the cell membranes but when there is an accumulation of cholesterol in the body, you can only imagine the damage it could cause from chest pain, arthrosclerosis to even death. Let us see how this happens. When there is a lot of cholesterol on your blood, they begin to deposit as fatty embolus or plaques on your blood vessels; this is like a sink wherein we do our dishes – as we wash our dishes daily and do not flush the sink with hot water and other treatments, with time, those oily substances will coagulate and clog the pipe making it difficult for water to pass through easily. Do you understand that picture? That is exactly what happens in your body, your blood vessels as the pipes over the years begin to be clogged by those fatty substances, making the lumen of these blood vessels narrower – now because they are narrower because of the blockage by a fatty embolus, it can lead to ischemia of a particular tissue being supplied by that blood vessel; further more if blood does not reach certain tissues because of lack of perfusion or a blocked blood vessel – the cells in the tissue begins to die – infarction. Also as a result of the fatty substances clogging the blood vessels, there is an impedance of blood flow, blood is coming from the heart, but it cannot flow out easily through certain arteries because of cholesterol blockage, hence the blood pressure in the body begins to increase – hypertension. Just picture a pipe carrying water from one place to another in a relatively high speed, then you block a part of the pipe, you will notice that pressure builds there, as this pressure increases it may exceed the elastic limit of the pipe leading to a collapse or breakage of the pipe causing the water in it to spill! This happens in the human body as blood pressure builds over a long period of time – the walls of the blood vessels collapse – Aneurysm, and then the content of the vessels spill – hemorrhages (if it is blood spilling) or exudates (if it is white blood cells, minerals and other content of the blood). And you know what all these do not end well! Depending on where these blockages happen it can lead to a heart attack or stroke – they are mostly fatal. Please beware, high cholesterol in the blood has no symptoms, it can only be detected when you carry out a blood test to check your blood cholesterol level.

It is true a tendency for having high cholesterol levels in the blood can be inherited, but it is 90 percent subject to lifestyle, choices and feeding. Come to think of it fruits, vegetables, legumes, nuts, grains, seed and water have zero cholesterol content! Feeding on whole plant based diets would be saving your life! I know you love yourself enough to save your life. In later segments of this book, I will show you a variety of very delicious and mouth watering meals that are easy to prepare. Do not get scared; you are not being sentenced to a strict vegan life like you are an Asian monk – you will enjoy every part of having a whole plant based diet!

Here are plant based foods substances that can help bring down your blood cholesterol especially the one referred to as low density lipoproteins (LDL) or bad cholesterol and probably increase your high density lipoproteins (HDL) or good cholesterol. Before we get into the foods, let us make a quick detour and understand what an LDL and a HDL is. Low Density Lipoproteins (LDL) or bad cholesterol are the nuisance that carries cholesterol all around the body, depositing them in blood vessels and subsequently causing damage over time. Whereas the High Density Lipoproteins (HDL) also called good cholesterol, pick up excess cholesterol and take them back to the liver for more metabolisms.

Back to food that can help you reduce the LDL or bad cholesterol in your blood;

Whole grains e.g Barley; this group of food substances reduce the cholesterol content in the blood by the soluble fiber they deliver.

Oats and oat meals; taking oats or a cold oat based cereals can drastically reduce bad cholesterol levels in the blood adding banana or strawberries to it will give you great effect in reducing blood cholesterol content because of the high fiber content they supply.

Beans; the beauty of beans apart from the fact that it is rich in soluble fiber is that it takes a longer time to digest – therefore it makes your body feel full for a longer time that means you will not feel like eating for a longer time so you will reduce cholesterol intake and at the same time deal with the metabolism of cholesterol in your blood from the soluble fiber that came from the beans. Apart from beans there are other legumes in the beans family, they also have the same effect on your body eg lentils, peas et cetera.

Okra and egg plants; these vegetables help control blood cholesterol levels as a result of their high soluble fiber content.

Nuts; almonds, peanuts, groundnuts, Brazil nuts and other nuts have been proven to be very good for the heart. So these nuts apart from their other health benefits are also good for the heart.

Vegetable oils; using vegetable oils rather than fats or butter for cooking our meals drastically lower low density lipoproteins or bad cholesterol.

Apples and citruses; have you ever heard, apples are good for your heart? It is because these contain a very high level of pectin which lowers low density lipoproteins.

Soy; food from soy for example, soybeans and soymilk, tofu are known to drastically bring down cholesterol content of the blood – taking about 25 grams of soy products daily has been proven to reduce blood low density lipoproteins by about 6%.

Fishes; eating fishes at least 3 times in a week will reduce your blood cholesterol content in two strategic ways; first by replacing meats which contain saturated fats and high cholesterol. Secondly by introducing omega-3-fatty acids which reduce triglycerides and thereby reducing the formation of low density lipoproteins. Omega-3-fatty acids are also good for the heart.

HELPS BURN FAT AND REDUCE OBESITY

A person is said to be obese when their body mass index (BMI) is above 30. It happens that one of the most important risk factor to diabetes and hypertension is obesity, but good news is, having a whole plant based diet together with exercises would help you cut down some fat.

Remember we have said that plant based diet have no cholesterol content, so it looks like a good first step to stepping down your weight; though there are other factors like exercise and the time of the day you eat. And also we have mentioned the effect beans has on your body, because of the slow rate at which it is digested – it can make you feel full for sometime cutting down your appetite for food for a long. A study carried out for 16 weeks showed how that plant based diet given to the cohort reversed their bodys to insulin; this reversal was seen to be brought about by plant protein.

A WHOLE PLANT BASED DIET PROVIDES YOU WITH UNPORCESSED FOOD WITH THE NUTIRENTS INTACT!

As we know generally food preparation processes that subject food to a lot of heat are prone to cause a lot of nutritional loss; and also majority of plant based meals do not need a lot of cooking! So a lot of the nutrients that should be in the food remain intact, especially the proteins and vitamins that are denatured by heat. This is a great health benefit of whole plant based diet. Do not misunderstand me, cooking food is good at least for the fact that the heat helps kill some microbes in the food – but more nutrients are also preserved by less cooking.

More to this is processed food, when we say "processed" we are talking about food that has gone through industrial scale procedures, having a lot of artificial flavors and sweeteners to make them palatable. So processed food will include food substances that are made with some artificial ingredients; therefore in our parlance, we are saying processed food in the light of being chemically processed rather than mechanically processed – because truthfully everything we eat is processed in a way. Some disadvantages in processed food;

They are mostly always heavy in processed sugar and fructose – corn syrup; when these are consumed in excess (of which they have a very addictive nature) they have very devastating effects. In as much as they have no calories, they can lead to insulin resistance in the body. High amounts of low density lipoprotein or bad cholesterol production in the body, increased triglycerides and increased fat accumulation in the abdomen, liver and kidney –leading to putting on of stubborn weight and maybe obesity. It is not news that the big four killer diseases are strongly linked to processed sugar; diabetes, heart diseases, hypertension and cancer.

They are made to become an addiction; the way processed food are created, are made to cause a production of dopamine when they are eaten making them to become an addiction – so in addition to the fact that they are unhealthy, they can be difficult to detach from; we begin to have a sense of I cannot do without these, therefore the earlier we move to whole plant based meals diets the better for us.

They contain an awful amount of artificial ingredients; in processed foods, there are a lot of colorants, texturants, preservatives, sweeteners, flavor et cetera and all these things are artificial ingredients added to processed food! Of course when you look at the average label of a processed food, you will notice many complex chemical names that you have no idea what they are, it is because they are all synthetic. Come to think of it, the producers of a certain food substance, will always keep their flavors secret, and for all I care that distinct flavor can be a combination of many chemicals – so we need to really cut down or even stop eating processed food, our lives depend on this switch to whole plant base diet.

They are often packed with refined carbohydrates; we know that carbohydrates from whole foods are way better and healthier than carbohydrates from refined food. Now the thing about refined carbohydrates is that they are quite simple and way easier to be broken down in the digestive tracts than their natural counterparts, so because of this ease in being broken down, they cause a spikes of sugar in our blood, which in turn causes a spike in insulin level in the blood – so the individual keeps having troughs and crests of hyperglycemia and hypoglycemia; so the blood sugar goes very high, and when there is a rapid secretion of insulin in the blood, the individual begins to crave sugar again because of the hypoglycemia that insulin has brought about, this instability in blood sugar is really unhealthy

They are always low in vitamins and minerals; industries that are focused on processed food are more interested in their profits than your health – quote me anywhere! What it may cost to make sure the necessary nutrients are in the food produced might be too high for the populace to easily purchase, so they produce low quality, low nutrients foods making them affordable in a large scale and make their profits. Moreover the processes that these food substances go through may lead to a loss of or denaturing of important nutrients. Finally there are trace elements and nutrients that natural sources have that science have not even conceived how to make in the laboratories – hence they cannot be found in processed food.

They are low in fiber; processed food are always low in fiber especially water soluble fiber which plays a very important role in cutting down bad cholesterol and building good cholesterol.

They require very little time to digest; this right here is quite dangerous, once they are broken down and digested – you begin to feel hungry again! And of course you will eat again – simply put, processed food is the short cut to weight gain and obesity. When you eat processed food, you will notice that they quickly calm your hunger but in very little time you are hungry again and craving something; therefore they become very addictive, as well as dangerous. This can lead to diabetes and other metabolism related diseases.

Processed food contains a lot of unhealthy fat; this quite unhealthy and keeps the hear at risk – these unhealthy fat increase the production of triglycerides and low density lipoproteins (bad cholesterol) increasing the risk of hypertension and cardiac diseases.

CHAPTER 2: OTHER BENEFITS OF HAVING PLANT-BASED MEALS

Plant-based meals have come a long way and more and more restaurants are embracing plant-based options. Gradually, the plant-based community has expanded. As the world keeps evolving, the need for plant-based food choices become more prominent. We have looked at all the health benefits of going plant-based, from a reduction in the risk of the occurrence of a heart disease, reduction of the risk of diabetes, energy boost and weight loss.

It is true that sticking with just plant produce will cause you to have a healthier and longer life. It will amaze you how much and how fast you will develop a healthy weight, a healthy mental state and a healthy skin. Eating plant-based meals may seem ordinary, but it has the capacity to affect every part of your life, and that of your environment. These and a few others are some of the other benefits we will look at, aside the obvious health perks.

Wellness goes beyond just our personal health and satisfaction. The environment and every other living thing should be involved in the goal of wellness. It is true that plant-based diets are fast becoming the popular kind of diet choice. However, these choices have less to do style and more to do with quality. Below are other reasons you should choose plant-based meals over animal-based meals.

For easy understanding, I will classify these benefits into personal and environmental.

PERSONAL BENEFITS;IT SAVES COST

Taking a break from all the talk about animals and the planet, cutting cost is another benefit of eating plant-based meals. I know you probably thought that eating plant-based meals are expensive, but nothing could be further from the truth. Plant-based ingredients are some of the cheapest ingredients to get from the store, and yes, they are usually cheaper than animal-based meals.

Okay, I will prove it. You know how much a package of tempeh costs? It is about three dollars. Same goes for a package of tofu. A pound of chicken (quality), on the other hand, is close to seven dollars. Same goes for quality beef and fresh fish. A fillet of fish costs more than a head of broccoli. Eggs are basically the only animal-based protein that are as cheap as plant-based ones, and maybe ground turkey. Vegan meals are often made up of legumes, grains. These items can be purchase in large quantities and stored at home for whenever you need to make something. If you are a smart shopper, you can also save lots of money on vegetables.

If you still do not believe me, then go eat out one of these days and check out the menu of the restaurant. You will find that the vegan options are usually cheaper than the animal food options. It is unbelievable that people actually think they are saving more money eating at McDonalds, when eating plant-based meals will make you spend even less than you would at McDonalds! Lets look at a typical McDonalds four-people meal– Chicken nuggets (six-piece), one small hamburger, two Big Macs, four medium drinks, four medium French fries. All of that will cost about twenty-four dollars.

Now, let us take a look at how much it will cost you to feed four people with a plant-based meal; salad, fruit, lentil soup and maybe sparkling mineral water will altogether cost only about ten dollars!

One of the best things about vegan food is that while it is cheap, it can last over a few days if properly refrigerated. In the end, you would have spent less than twenty dollars on food for a few days. You could make a large pot of soup and have for lunch and even dinner for a few days and would have saved yourself the time you would have used to make another dish. The cheapest foods in the market include lentils, beans, fruits and vegetables.

IT LETS YOU GET YOUR CREATIVE JUICES FLOWING
Eating plant-based meals give you an opportunity to get creative with your meals. You know how you eat some meals for a while and you are really fed up with the routine? Almost like your taste buds and cooking skills are in search of an adventure. Switching to plant-based meals will mean that you would have to go outside the box most of the time if you are going to make really good plant-based meals. You could search the internet for lots of vegetarian ideas or even come up with yours. It is always exciting to try out one or two new things in the kitchen.

BETTER SEX

If no other benefit gets your attention, this probably will (winks). You see, with plant-based meals, you are getting a variety of nutrients. Enough of these nutrients are not just good for your health; they will also boost your sex life. For example, did you know that zinc boosts the production of testosterone? Of course, you know that an increase production of testosterone means an increase in stamina and sexual desire. Guess what foods are rich in zinc; Pumpkin seeds and chickpeas. Another example is vitamin B. The B vitamins influence the release of sex hormones into the body. A body that lacks vitamin B will get lethargic, and this translates to a low sex-drive. Guess what foods contain vitamin B; lentils, bananas and beans.

These are only little examples of the numerous other nutrients and vitamins that are important for a healthy sex life. Basically, eat as many colors of these foods as they usually contain different nutrients necessarily for the proper functioning of the important organs.

HELPS RELAX YOUR BODY

Plants are good sources of melatonin, tryptophan and serotonin. These are neurotransmitters which help in the reduction of stress and anxiety, will improving relaxation of the body. Tryptophan can be found in potatoes and beans, tomatoes, pineapples, bananas and plums are great sources of serotonin and seeds and fenugreek are rich sources of melatonin.

YOU WOULD BE WALKING IN THE FOOTSTEPS OF OTHER GREAT PEOPLE

I bet you did not know, but a lot of really popular people are on plant-based diets. We are talking Beyoncé, Jay Z, Miley Cyrus, Liam Hemsworth, Ariana Grande, Jennifer Lopez, Ellen DeGeneres, Portia de Rossi, Ellie Goulding. Of course, thats why they look the way they do! If this is not a light bulb moment for you, I do not know what will.

Lots of other great people like Denzel Washington, Leonardo Da Vinci, Betty White, Albert Einstein, Jane Goodall, Mahatma Ghandi, Rosa Parks and Leo Tolstoy. Of course, there are other amazing people and I cant mention all of their names.

The point, though, is that if youre making a choice to switch to the plant-based diet option, then you are in the best company!

WILL HELP CLEAR UP YOUR ACNE

Truth is, you would hardly stick to plant-based meals and have acne breakouts. These breakouts are often caused by the saturated fats that come from the consumption of animal products, especially dairy products. These saturated fats are not entirely healthy and go on to clog your skin pores, leading to breakouts, blackheads and a lot of other skin problems. It is best to stick with plant-based meals because apart from how they contain no saturated fats and will not clog your skin pores, they also contain nutrients and pigments that are good for the skin.

YOU WILL SLEEP BETTER

One of the most important requirements for good sleep is balanced nutrition. This, you can get from eating lots of vegetables and fruits. When your body is consistently supplied with these important nutrients, it has the necessary materials to do all of the things it should do, like replacing old and worn out cells with better cells and reducing the stress hormone (cortisol) levels in the body. A reduction in cortisol levels will help the body get rested and relaxed enough to sleep better.

Apart from the reduction of cortisol levels, balanced nutrition from plant-based meals will also curb your cravings, that way; you will not be craving stuff that can inhibit your sleep like carbonated or caffeinated sodas and processed sugars.

YOU WILL BE ABLE TO THINK MORE CLEARLY

Processed foods are highly unhealthy and are sometimes the reason you cannot think clearly. Typically, when digestion is inefficient in the body, it causes the body to expend a lot of energy trying to digest food. This can cause you to not think clearly as your energy is being diverted elsewhere. But, eating plant-based meals mean efficiency in digestion which in turn mans that your body saves energy so that you think clearly.

HEALTHY SKIN, NAILS AND HAIR
Avoiding meat, dairy and processed food, and sticking to a healthy plant-based diet will reflect on your skin, your eyes, your nails and your hair. It will cause these parts of your body to glow naturally; you would wonder how it is all happening. Plus, this is by far the cheapest and easiest way to get glowing skin, nails and hair. All of the processed foods contain unhealthy stuff like saturated fat and toxins that are unhealthy for the skin, especially.

Plants possess a detoxifying effect, elimination benefits and are easily digestible. This means that your body gets to deal with fewer toxins. Toxins are usually responsible for acne, eye bags and dull skin. Plus, since plant-based foods are a lot easier to digest, this means that the body does not have to spend so much energy and time trying to digest, thus, giving more time and energy for beautifying.

Plant-based meals, especially vegetables and fruits are rich in vitamins that aid in the beautifying of the body. For example, vitamin C contained in sweet potatoes boosts the production of collagen and helps to reduce the appearance of wrinkles. Lycopene, found in tomatoes help to keep the skin protected from the potential damage of the sun. Other nutrients found in plants that help keep the skin healthy includes beta-carotene and lutein, they help to keep the skins oft and supple.

GIVES YOU A BIT OF AN EXCITEMENT AND SAVES TIME

If you are used to making animal-based meals, cooking plant-based ones may seem intimidating. But there is absolutely nothing to worry about. Cooking would not automatically be difficult because there is no dairy or meat. What you get instead is a whole new world of excitement trying to find new and interesting recipes to try out.

Plant-based meals are usually pretty straightforward, which means more time saved. For example, it would not take you long to make coconut curry or even bean stew. Not to mention all the fun spices and flavors, there are more than twenty thousand edible plant species in the world. The thought of trying out new dishes should excite you especially if you are an adventure lover.

YOU WILL BECOME HAPPIER

Animal-based foods affect your hormones. You see, when an animal is about to be killed, just like humans, they also produce stress hormones. These stress hormones will get ingested when you eat that animal, causing all kinds of feelings like depression, anxiety, fatigue and even anger.

Plants, on the other hand, possess antioxidants, along with phytonutrients which are useful in the elevation of moods. These phytonutrients and antioxidants also help to combat illnesses associated with saturated fats, sugar and salts. So, imagine your life and your mood, when you eat plant-based foods!

ENVIRONMENTAL BENEFITS ;IT SUPPORTS THE ENVIRONMENT

Sustainability has been a hotly debated topic lately and we all should be taking this more seriously than we are. We should be accountable to earth as occupants here, and show this accountability by protecting the planet along with everybody and every animal on it. One of the biggest ways to protect the earth is by eating plant-based meals.

How do you mean? You might ask. Thirty-four thousand people had their diets investigated in a study and it was found that it was better for planet earth if people ate meals that were rich in vegetables and fruits, than consuming meals that were animal-based.

Did you know that animal agriculture is the cause of most of the greenhouse gas that is emitted? As a matter of fact, animal agriculture causes more greenhouse gas emission than the transportation sector. Yes, the whole transportation sector!

It is also responsible for about eighty percent of the Amazon deforestation and water wastage. The dairy and meat industry use up to one-third of the earths fresh water. Livestock takes up forty-five percent of land space. Eating a plant-based meal will save an animal, save carbon dioxide emissions and forest.

If you have been paying attention, then you know by now that our environment is in the middle of a wild crisis. All we should be aiming for is finding ways to cut down on how much harm we are causing to our environment by reducing the amount of dairy and meat we are consuming.

A few studies assert that if we adopt the plant-based diet, you can cut carbon footprints by fifty percent.

WILL SAVE ANIMALS

I feel that when people see some of the foods on the grocery shelves, their minds do not see that the food on the shelf was once a living animal. If people did make this connection, they would probably eat less of these animal-based foods. These animals are living beings with emotions and intellect; they understand, communicate, and feel suffering and happiness. It doesnt matter if they are reared in a free-range farm or industrial one. Eating a plant-based diet means that you are compassionate and are mindful of your relationship with the environment and with the animals that live on the planet with us. Of course, eating plant-based is beyond just your health and personal benefits, it is also about how aware and empathetic you are about your environment.

Apart from the fact that these animals are subjected to really horrific conditions, they are reared under heart-breaking conditions. Some get sick and little babies get separated from their mothers immediately they are born. Some sleep on their feces and I do not know what could be more horrific. In pigs, they are mostly artificially inseminated and placed in what is called gestation crates. These crates are often really small and the pigs are literally squeezed into such a tiny space throughout their pregnancy. As they grow, they may sometimes develop what sores referred to as pressure sores. There are little slots in the crates through which the pigs pass out feces and urine. The ammonia smell is horrible and is unhealthy for the lungs of even an animal. After delivery, the pig is artificially inseminated again and taken back to the gestation crate. These animals go through this cycle until they become almost useless, then they are slaughtered. This is done to save money and have more meat produced. Heartless, isnt it? Just writing about it stirs all kinds of emotions.

Learning about the conditions these animals are subjected to will make a person with a conscience think twice about eating animal-based foods. Animals are intelligent and have emotions too. They shouldnt have to go through this because of what humans can get from them. That is just selfish.

So, eating plant-based meals will mean that you have basically saved an animal or that you are not part of the animal cruelty and you are helping save the planet and its occupants.

WILL HELP PREVENT EXTINCTION OF SPECIES

Did you know that the major cause of extinction of species is animal agriculture? This, along with other horrible results like habitat destruction, ocean dead zones and the likes. It is also the reason the Amazon forest has deteriorated so badly. Every minute, more and more acres of rainforest, meant to be the home of different species, keep getting destroyed. Presently, over a hundred million acres have been cleared as a result of animal agriculture.

With the consistent destruction of the rainforest, more than a hundred species of animals, insects and even plants are lost, and no, not every year, every day! Apart from the habitat destruction, predators and those beautiful alpha species are often hunted down and killed to protect livestock and livestock profits. Plus, the livestock farmers have to use herbicides, pesticides and a host of chemical fertilizers to aid their crops meant for feeding livestock.

What is not considered in all of this is that these chemicals are harmful to the animal reproductive systems and can also poison animal water sources.

In the oceans, there is so much exploitation of the ocean species that has successfully depleted resources and species.

Eating plant-based meals would mean that you are a part of the minority that actually care about other species.

WILL HELP REDUCE WASTE POLLUTION

News flash; over seven million pounds of faeces are produced every minute by the animals reared for food! As a matter of fact, close to three thousand cows reared for dairy will produce same amount of waste a forty-one thousand people population would produce. What the heck! Yes, I thought so too. It is great if you care about stuff like this and sow it in your actions. Imagine if the world decided to go plant-based. Half of our environmental problems would literally be solved.

WILL HELP CURB DEFORESTATION

I already mentioned that close to ninety percent of the destruction of amazon is caused by animal agriculture. Every minute, at least an acre of land is cleared for the singular purpose of growing feed for livestock and grazing of the livestock. As a result, the planet grows more and more bereft of oxygen.

Will Solve the Issue of Hunger

The problem is not that enough food is not grown; the problem is that most of the food grown is used to feed livestock, instead of humans. Currently, food grown is enough to feed about ten billion people. The grain alone fed to livestock would be food for over eight hundred million people. So, you see, it is not a scarcity issue, it is an allocation issue.

According to a study done at Lancaster University, crops are already cultivated, ones enough to feed both the present world population and thirty years into the future! Another analysis similar to this says that the US could feed its entire citizen and close to four hundred million more people. It was noted that this would be possible if we all went plant-based.

Going plant-based would help prevent the killing of animals for food and will feed the one billion people who have close to nothing to eat. The animal-based food system is obviously doing more harm than good, taking up half the lands, emitting greenhouse gas and feeding livestock with half the crops cultivated, instead of feeding people.

WILL CONTRIBUTE TO WATER CONSERVATION

It would surprise you that majority of the water consumed in the United States alone goes to animal agriculture. As a matter of fact, a full third of the earths fresh water goes to the dairy and meat industry. It takes close to five hundred gallons of water to churn out a quarter pound of hamburger, just one. For dairy, it takes about a thousand gallons to produce a gallon of milk! You would agree that this is an unwise and inefficient way to produce food and at this rate, things would not look too great in the future.

HELPS CONSERVE LAND

I mentioned before that close to half of the earths land space has been covered by livestock. Basically, an acre and half are needed to produce close to four hundred pounds of meat. However, this same land can be used to produce thirty-seven thousand pounds of crops. What this means is that the person who eats meat will need eighteen times more land than the plant-based eater. How sick is that?

The world would be a better place if we all went plant-based, wouldnt it?

CHAPTEER 3: BURN FAT, LOSE WEIGHT AND GAIN ENERGY WITH PLANT BASED DIET

What is Obesity and being Overweight, and when is there a problem?

Overweight and obesity are defined as abnormal or excessive fat accumulation that may impair human health.
Being obese is as a result of inactivity, calorie to activity ratio. This simply means that taking high fat dense food and not exercising, or taking the stairs amongst other things will result to obesity or being overweight.

Is very easy to become overweight but the very funny thing is, its harder or more less seems to be harder to lose weight. Why is it so? This is because it takes more energy and can be time-consuming to actually keep your body at high level of activity thereby reducing the amount of excessive fat in your body. This is usually calculated using your body mass index.
Body mass index (BMI) is a simple index of weight-for-height that is majorly used to differentiate and tell who is overweight and obese and who isnt in adults. It is defined as a persons weight in kilograms divided by the square of his height in meters (kg/m2).
For adults, World Health Organization (WHO) defines overweight and obesity as follows:
Overweight is when a persons BMI is greater than or equal to 25; and
Obesity is ones BMI is greater than or equal to 30.
BMI = weight in kg/ (height in m) 2

A table is used to measure the BMI of an individual.
Less than 18.5 – Underweight
- 18.5 to 25 – Desirable or healthy range
- 25-30 – Overweight
- 30-35 – Obese (Class I)
- 35-40 – Obese (Class II)
- Over 40 – Morbidly or severely obese (Class III)

So let us say you weigh 68kg and your height is 7 feet 8 inches, you are most likely going to behave a BMI of 22.8kg/m2 which is considered normal, but if you weight say 92kg with the same height your BMI is most likely going to be 32.8 and you are considered OBESE.

Unlike before now, where obesity was linked to very developed countries, but now obesity has become a worldwide issue. It is not just linked to developed countries but now every country all around the world even some underdeveloped countries are suffering from obesity too. Some records claim that in every three adults one person is obese or overweight.

So if what could a persons body weight to be obese or overweight sometimes may not just be food and energy activity ratio, sometimes it is just family, genetics or even a persons environment.

It has been said that during the times when humans were evolving and evolution was taking place, most times there was scarcity of food which would take the humans days before the next meal is available, this made the human body grow up adapting to the fact that it had to store food for rainy days when humans went out to hunt for food so as to keep alive, we may call this a survival instinct.

This, we can confidently say might be the reason why food is stored in the human body as fat not knowing how to differentiate two different ages.

And even as a 21st century millennial living in this Era, where every single thing in the world right now are moving into automation the human body does not receive as much activity as it used to thereby making the fact of energy being stored to be in on the increase. More and more persons are getting obese even before you are done reading this book.

Being obese or overweight is an issue that can affect your health, your family as it has to do with your standard of living and even create more risks for you in the future. Some of the health related issues that an overweight or obese person suffers can lead to death, while some may leave you in and out of a health clinic every single day which is time consuming and energy killing.

Some of the major health related diseases with being overweight and obese are

*cardiovascular diseases (mainly heart disease and stroke), which were the leading cause of death in 2012;

*diabetes; tendencies to have this diesel are super high for those who are obese.

*musculoskeletal disorders (especially osteoarthritis – a highly disabling degenerative disease of the joints);

*some cancers (including endometrial, breast, ovarian, prostate, liver, gallbladder, kidney, and colon).

*Heart disease

Why do people gain weight?

Many things can be the cause of weight gain and can 100% affect how much weight your body can and will stores.

If you take in more calories from food or beverages than you use up in physical activity, movement here and there and through daily living, such as sitting or sleeping, your body stores the extra calories and keeps them as fat and if overtime, you continue to consume more in calories than you burn off throughout the day, you are most likely going to gain weight. Excessive weight gain may lead to overweight or obesity based on how we just calculated the Body Mass Index (BMI).

How does losing weight work?
It sounds like a math question right? More like, solve the perpendicular square foot of a circle (please do not even think of my math equation, it does not make sense).
So some people claim that their Weight is usually affected by their high or low metabolism and this affects them. Is this true? Does metabolism affect a persons weight?
Let us see!
Metabolism is the process by which your body converts whatever you eat or drink into energy. This would mean saying that the energy giving food you dear and drink converts to what your body uses to do work.
 During this complex biochemical process, the calories in your food and beverages are combined with oxygen to release the energy your body needs to function and go about daily activities.
Even when you are at sleep or at rest, your body still needs energy for all its unspoken and unseen functions, like breathing, circulating blood, adjusting hormone levels, growing and even when it is repairing cells. This function all require energy from your body and this energy is gotten from the food and drink you take during your time awake.
The amount of calories your body will use to carry out these basic and unseen functions can be known as your basal metabolic rate — what you might call metabolism.

People metabolism rate differs based on so many reasons, one of which is Different things can affect your metabolism or your metabolic rate all whilst either losing weight or adding. Some of which are;

Your Gender - males have a higher tendency of burning more calories than women who may be of the same, age, height and weight.

Your body composition : some persons who are bigger and have more muscles tend to burn more calories faster than regular people who are not in that categories.

Your Age also plays a role in metabolism and its rate. This shows that the older you get, the lesser calories your body tends to burn as it goes along the way.

Unfortunately, weight gain is a complicated process just like the math above.

Its just a combination of little algebras we may never get like genetic makeup, hormonal controls, diet composition and the impact of environment on your lifestyle, including sleep, physical activity and stress, a whole lot constitutes the whole idea of weight gain.

The logic is very simple you gain weight when your body makes use of fewer calories than you actually eat or when your body burns lower calories than you eat.

So looking at it losing weight, this will only mean as long as you make sure that your calorie level intake is low compared to the calories level you burn as energy or you burn more calories than you eat you will be on your way to that body you have always dreamed about.

Let us put it in simple math, if you burn 2000 calories per day according your metabolic rate which includes all energy to use up in a day including passive energy and you eat in a day 2500 calories from your daily food intake, what do you think happens to the 500 calories that is left? Quick answer, it stays in your body as fat and if this is repetitive – you will store more fat than your body should take. Then again, let us say you eat 1000 calories in a day and your body uses only about 2000 calories in a day, you would see that you will lose more weight and even faster. Have you seen that it is little wonder some persons actually take note of calories intake per day, so they can say how many calories is needed at that point in time according to their metabolic rate. They are even smart watches that have been made for that and have calories checker in them.

While it is true that some persons seem to be able to lose weight more quickly and more easily than others, everyone loses weight when they burn up more calories than they eat.

Let me refresh your memory again on the basics, because from repetition I will drive this to your subconscious – What is a plant based diet?

A plant-based diet is a diet consisting mostly or entirely of foods derived from plants, including vegetables, grains, nuts, seeds, legumes and fruits, and with few or no animal products. A plant based-diet is not necessarily a vegetarian diet, but rather means that you are choosing to rightly proportion your food with more plant based food – of course remember what the idea is, I am not trying to make you vegan, but to make you have mostly plant based food, little animal food, and zero tolerance for processed food. A person who takes a plant based diet might occasionally want to eat meat and the likes, this just only means that your diet is perhaps a heavy percentage filled up with plant-based products than on meat and dairy products. It focuses on unprocessed foods, specifically plants, and is effective at stimulating weight loss and improving health

As much as there is always confusion as to how a plant-based diet and some persons will choose to occasionally take meat and uses educational binge while some other person takes meat and uses it as toppings or in very low quantity of plant-based diets

Some of the major characteristics of a plant-based diet are as follows

1. Emphasizes whole, minimally processed foods.
2. Limits or avoids animal products.
3 Focus on plants, including vegetables, fruits, whole grains, legumes, seeds and nuts, which should make up the majority of what you eat. Refined diet promoting locally sourced, organic food whenever possible

So lets look at some of the major categories when it comes to plant based diet

Fruits: These would include any type of fruit like apples, bananas, grapes, strawberries, citrus fruits, et cetera.
Vegetables: plenty of vegetables including peppers, corn, avocados, lettuce, spinach, kale, peas, collards, etc are great plant based diet contributors
Tubers: Also root vegetables are amazing great like potatoes, carrots, parsnips, sweet potatoes, beets, etc.
Whole grains: grains, cereals, and other starches in their whole form, such as quinoa, brown rice, millet, whole wheat, oats, barley, etc. Even popcorn is a whole grain
Legumes: This would include beans of any kind, plus lentils, pulses, and similar ingredients
It may seem difficult at first when stating up in the plant based world, over time, eating a plant-based diet will become second nature.

HOW TO LOSE WEIGHT ON A PLANT DIET

A plant-based diet to me following some ground rules which are very easy to follow if you consistently follow them.
Having at the back of your mind the fact that read as much as possible even though do they do not contribute 100% to your weight loss but he has to role to play remember the maths the number of calories you taken a number of expanded energy that happens.
So how do we lose weight on a plant-based diet?

EAT THREE MEALS A DAY

Secular point is very key only like what people think where they stink starving yourself of a meal or two sure way of losing weight this is not true remember to Nowhere your body begins to store food as fat simply because it feels is going into when you are hungry that is what happens when you skip meals he is very important in losing weight but now youre not just eating three Square meals of everything that you can see youre eating three Square meals of whole products we are talking about avoiding by all means processed carbohydrates and sugar as much as possible.

DIDNT MOMMY TEACH YOU TO HAVE BREAKFAST?

Many people do not know that the reason why they are adding flesh is because they are starving! "Well, I thought that should have been the reason why I would lose weight?" they say. Truth is, that is not how it works; and I will show you briefly.
First off, skipping breakfast keeps you hungry throughout the day unconsciously making the temptation of snacking very high! So you keep nibbling on those high calorie junks and then, voila! After few months – you are fat (I wanted to add like a pig, but I did not say it).

Secondly, it is easier for your body to digest and metabolize three small meals that 2 larger ones. When we take those smaller meals, they are easily made available for the body to burn it! But the two larger meals take more work for the body to break down and make available for us to use, therefore they are stored in the adipose tissues and you know what that means – fat! You know it is like trying to burn a chunk of wood in comparism to when you want to burn saw dust of the same weight; the saw dust would burn faster – that is the picture I am trying to paint for you here, so instead of eating lets say 4kg of food twice a day (that is 2kg per meal) because of how hungry you are, why not break it down to 1kg + 2kg + 1kg (breakfast lunch and dinner respectively)

You see in the other of priority, your brain wants to survive more than it wants you to look beautiful; even in Abraham Maslows hierarchy of needs; the most basic needs are forged by our instincts for survival. That said, when you think you will lose weight by starving, your brain will switch gears using a feedback loop mechanism for you to survive – let us explain it in the simplest terms. There are two major hormones for hunger and appetites: the first one, Leptin is responsible for reducing appetite. The second one is Gherin, this hormone increases appetite, so it seems this hormone increases your feeling of hunger. Now when we eat and we are full, messages are sent to the brain which in turn sensitizes your fatty cells to secrete Leptin, causing you to feel like not eating any longer. After three hours, the body begins to secrete gherin again – hence it is called a loop. Now, if you are in a habit of starving yourself to lose weight, after sometime your brain would increase the secretion of leptin (which reduces the feeling of hunger or shuts down your appetite) to cope with the stress of starvation – do you understand the reverse psychology your brain is playing with you just to cope with the stress of starvation? When the body keeps producing leptin for a long time as a result of our habitual starvation or missing of breakfast, the loop for appetite also sensitizes the body to be slow in breaking down fat – because leptin is produced by fatty cells; hence making the body fat persistent – why? Your brain wants to survive. If I was your brain right now youll hear "I dont wanna die, I dont care how ugly you look, nah nah nah nah nah nah!" So do you get the picture? You thought by starving you will lose weight; it began to work and boom! There was a reverse, your brain switched to survival mode rather than beauty mode and makes the fat stick with you at the same time reducing your bodys ability to burn fat!

So what is the way forward? Take protein and "fat" filled meals as breakfast! Yes, you saw right! These food classes, stick longer in your stomach and make you less likely to feel hungry in a long while, secondly, fatty foods help the body produce leptin which reduces your appetite for eating. So first thing in this journey of losing weight in 14 days is – TAKE YOUR BREAK FAST AND STOP STARVING.

Hey, stop snacking. Yes, for the next fourteen days in this journey, do not snack. The thing about snacks is; they have very high sugar and calorie content but do not satisfy you, so you keep taking them and you are actually taking an enormous amount of sugar and calorie in those precious bites of goodness (LOL)… but you know what? Drink more water! Should I break your head again about the benefits of water? I would have swung into my scientific mode, but I promised you: no scientific horrors and no jaw-breaking statistics. So trust and follow, we will walk through this together. Just drink water, breathe and drink a little bit more. Water has zero sugar, zero calories but it has the ability to temporarily fill your stomach; thereby reducing the potential of your stomach lining producing more gherin which would make you feel hungry; and by so doing, you just pushed back a potential of taking a snack, and taking in more calories. So, breathe and drink! Keep snacking to a minimum and eat fruit. Fruits are a great way to get fiber and high nutrient intake plus they have a good taste in the mouth at least most of them like apples oranges pineapples and the likes what you take food as often as possible and snack on them even if you have to do this as daily

More so, you may not know that why you put up excess weight is because you eat very late at night! Look, even for a person with normal metabolism, good weight and probably their dream body – the last meal of the day should be eaten at least 3 hours before you go to bed! Now for those of us that really want to lose weight; you need to go the extra 2 miles. If you are a person that sleeps by 10pm, make sure you have your last meal by 6pm and do not snack! When you wake up in the morning have your breakfast – it is better to have three small meals a day than to yank in 2 large meals! In fact depending on how fat you are, you need to make your last meal at least 4 hours before you sleep. If you are diabetic, you need to discuss this with your doctor. An obese person on the other hand needs to eat their last meal 6 hours before bed time! This will give your body time to burn those calories – simple right? But it is not easy. It will put your discipline level to the test.

Finally, after each meal, do not lie down immediately. Come on, sit for some time, and walk for some time. I know when you are full it comes with that slight feeling of tiredness as a result of the spiking and dipping of your blood sugar level, well, this is where you need your discipline – sit or stand or walk – basically, I am saying you have to position yourself in a way that gravity would work directly on the food in accordance to your peristaltic movement. This also would put your discipline to the test. This seems simple right? But this is actually not easy.

EAT WHOLE GRAINS AS PRIMARY FOOD.

There is a huge difference between whole grains and process carbohydrate or simple sugars is very important that one gets to know what is what and which is Which to avoid issues that may arise as a result of not knowing. Some examples are: brown rice, quinoa, and millet. Sometimes cracked grains are included in healthy diets as well, but limit those cracked grains to once a day or every other day if you are trying to lose weight just like your bread even though its written whole grain, it is a cracked grain.

Eat beans, and its products: do this at least once a day, and if you are hungry eat them twice a day. Beans (without a ton of oil) are very low in fat and very high in fiber and nutrients. Some examples are chickpeas, black beans, tofu, tempeh, and lentils -- just to name a few!

AVOID PROCESSED FOODS

Avoiding processed food will actually mean what it is avoiding processed food that would mean its getting rid of every quick kind of food you have in your refrigerator one of the easiest way to actually add weight or not lose weight is actually eating processed food because those filled actually filled with things that you do not have to have in your body

ALWAYS START WITH A SALAD

Usually it is good to start with a salad why because it ensures that you are actually taking a good number of required vitamins and minerals in your body work for the day so helps fill you up faster so that at the time when the main food would come youre already full Intels your body that you are satisfied a simple trick that works

SPICE THINGS UP

I would like to Spice things up putting a whole lot of chili pepper in your meals will help make you feel up and satiated faster and better. Black pepper, meanwhile, contains a substance called piperine — and research has revealed that piperine can help the body burn more calories through the process of thermogenesis

ALWAYS MAKE YOUR MEALS BEFORE HAND

It is easier when you already have food cooked and packed when you trying to lose weight on a plant-based diet than actually always trying to prepare your food when you are hungry; most likely you would want to binge on processed food so it is always advisable to have batch cooking, cooking on the weekends when you have a lot more time to spare than rush cooking each time you want to eat. Not a great move!

EAT VEGETABLES OF ALL KINDS

Spitting vegetables are very good and they are high in nutrient. Also keep you filled up and makes you feel satisfied. So it becomes a win-win situation. Try a variety of leafy vegetables such as kale, collards, Swiss chard, spinach, and other greens each day. Steam, grill, braise, or stir-fry to preserve their flavor and nutrients.
You do not have to avoid meat. You do not have to really avoid eating meat. You can actually change the way you think about meat using it or having it in smaller amounts. Use it as a garnish instead of a centerpiece.

Choose fats, but the good ones. Yes it is good for you to avoid oil and actually use them in little quality but then you can actually go for very good oils to. Fats in olive oil, olives, nuts and nut butters, seeds, and avocados are particularly healthy choices. Use this one instead of using the over saturated fat filled oils out there.

Be a Vegetarian for one night. It is good for you to consciously and actually create new plants that surrounds what you are trying to achieve it be advisable that at least once in a week you consciously say you want to eat vegetable based products. Be a vegetarian for one day. It is important that these meals are made around beans, whole grains, and vegetables.

A WHOLE GRAIN BREAKFAST CHOICE

This is good for you to actually consciously make these products that actually plant-based to be added to your every single waking eating moment from to lunch to dinner to desert and every single thing that you put in your mouth. Start with oatmeal, quinoa, buckwheat, or barley. Then add some nuts or seeds along with fresh fruit.

Use only small amounts of oil in cooking is better to use little or no oil if possible very high in fat very much processed. So avoiding oil as often as possible is a great way to keep up with a plant based diet. Understand that people who follow a plant-based diet tend to have lower body mass indexes (BMIs) when calculated compared to those who are on the other end counterparts. Studies have shown that people who use a vegetarian diet to lose weight are more successful not only at dropping pounds, but also at keeping them off as this is quite important in any weight loss process. Following a plant based diet helps keep you full, avoiding binging for you and keeping your metabolism rate stable against your calorie intake thereby making it absolute necessary and possible to lose weight and keep it off. This isnt starving and eating only green vegetables all day long, No. This is more like, enjoying a long term process where occasionally meat and other products can come in but a majority of your diet will be only plant based food.

EXERCISES THAT HELP WEIGHT LOSS ON A PLANT BASED DIET

While it is very important that you actually change your diet and actually take note of your eating habits with the plant-based diet. It is also important that you understand that exercise is important to the overall weight loss of any individual. Exercise is important because just like your metabolism rate where your bodys rate at which it consumes and changes it to energy is quite low, exercise becomes that bridge that helps you triple your metabolism rate and makes all that calories that you have taken in to be expended out and even more.

There are major exercises you can actually do to lose a certain number of calories per day
Mountains climber 641 calories
Ski jumps 520 calories

Burpees 380 calories
Skipping 640 calories
Jumping Jacks 520 calories
Squash - 886 calories
Running - 738 calories
Rugby - 738 calories
Martial Arts - 738 calories
Skipping - 738 calories
Boxing - 664 calories
BMX or Mountain Biking - 627 calories
Swimming - 591 calories
Rock Climbing - 591 calories
Football - 591 calories

As there are exercises that help lose calories faster, so are there others that arent as effective even though this solely dependent on your needs alone.
Top ten exercises that burn the least calories
1. Yoga - 185 calories
2. Surfing - 221 calories
3. Pilates - 221 calories
4. Sailing / Windsurfing - 221 calories
5. Weightlifting - 221 calories
6. Walking - 244 calories
7. Table Tennis - 295 calories
8. Gymnastics - 295 calories
9. Horse Riding - 295 calories
10. Golf - 332 calories

CONCLUSION

Obesity is never a good thing so been able to solve that problem and doing it with plant-based products is actually a very good thing it is very possible early on weight losing weight face products very possible it is advisable that most times you calculate your body Max index and that weight under the 25 so as to curtail the kind of food you eat the kind of kind of places and exercises should do so as to help maintain do for your body also learning to keep the weight away one major for anyone who is looking to lose weight it takes a whole lot to lose weight but you can expand half the energy trying to keep off the weight. So most times youd have to consciously and deliberately follow through your plant diet controls occasionally take meat products but majorly keeping your diet on a 100% plant based produce.

Always putting in mind that your BMI determines your weight decisions and can help be a directive as to what you should be doing and how you can improve on what you are doing already.

Underweight is a BMI less than 18.5

Normal weight is a BMI between 18.5 and 24.9

Overweight is a BMI of 25 to 29.9

Obesity is a BMI of 30 or greater

In conclusion, changing your life decisions might just be push you need to get better physically and look healthier and younger too. So taking in considerations, your metabolism rate, the intake your of calories your body need, genetics and also environmental factors you can be able to ascertain how the plant based diet would be good for you and how often you should take it, and also how much of the plant-based diet you are willing to follow through. Also putting in mind the enormous advantages that there is in following a plant based diet like improving your overall weight and also health, it is without a doubt that the plant based diet is good for anyone willing to change his or her health.

HOW TO GAIN ENERGY WITH PLANT BASED DIET

If you have ever seen an athlete running or perhaps children playing around and you have wondered how "if only I had that kind of energy the things I would do" well maybe we need to work on changing your diet. One of the primary ways we gain our energy is from fatty foods, or what we call fats and oils. They are found from animals sources (mostly the fats) and plant sources (mostly the oils). But in this chapter what I seek to point out to you is how you can have all the energy you need from healthy oils that come from plant sources – these are healthier and safer!

You have no idea of what great Advantages of having a plant-based diet and letting go of animal-based Diet can afford you; this is one topic that is too wide and too deep to truly understand. But remember of course the idea here is not to make you vegan – I seek to point you to a life style where you feed mostly on plant based food substances, little animal based food substances and no tolerance for processed or refined food, and by refined we do not mean mechanical processing but chemical processing.

If you have ever been the one person that coffee makes you come alive, and you will need to pop pills (supplements) before you start the day, then perhaps you just need to have a change of diet plan.

What is the one thing that the game changer and can make you gain more energy to be able to be more productive, energized and to be able to start your day on a good foot; the real magic is consuming whole plant based foods, which constitutes of a powerhouse of nutrients to keep you moving.

When you eliminate excessive animal products from your diet, and take no processed food at all may shock you, it does magic. It can lighten the workload on your entire system and make you feel lighter and more energized. This workload lightening translates to more energy for you.

Even professional athletes are moving toward changing diets to plant based food because of the enormous advantages you can derive from them.

Many people can feel and become tired or run-down at some point during the day and even some before the beginning of the day. A lack of energy can affect your daily activities and these in turn can make you more or less productive.

The fact is that the type of food and even the quantity of food you eat can play an essential role in determining your energy level during and after each day.

Sticking to the plant based diet may just be the only step to changing how to wake up daily, how you go through the day and how you end the day, very dependent on what you take into the body.

Even though all foods give you energy, some foods contain nutrients that could help increase your energy levels and maintain your alertness and focus throughout the day.

SO HOW DOES IT WORK?

One of the major differences between fatty acids or lipids found in plants and those found in animals might be due to additional vitamins found within these food substances, they contain certain other nutrients; monosaturated fats of plant origins are really rich in vitamins, and also contain polysaturated fats which are generally known to be good for the heart. Fats of animal sources on the other hand contain saturated fats and cholesterol is dangerous to the heart and the blood vessels. Now these monosaturated fats we talked about are found in olives, nuts, avocados as well as white meats and dairy products. Though studies have shown that monosaturated fats are good for the heart, other studies refute this thesis – but all the same, studies that show that monosaturated fats are good for the heart exceed contrary studies.

The fatty foods we eat are not as important as their sources, because the source of the fatty food you eat makes the difference. Academic studies carried out in Havard on 90,000 individuals, the cohort were watched for an average of 22 years – it was discovered that risks of heart diseases were reduced when plant based monosaturated fat, were used to replace unhealthy and unsaturated fat, refined sugars and trans fat. It was discovered that feeding on plant based fats brought about 16% reduction in the risk of mortality from any cause; whereas eating of animal based fats was seen to be responsible for a 21% increase in risk of dying from any cause. Now do not get me wrong; you do not need to totally take away fat from your food, of course certain fats are very great for our health, for example, certain vitamins need to be dissolved in fats for them to be properly metabolized; these are called fat soluble vitamins. So my emphasis here is that you focus on plant based lipids or oils.

Note that there are different types of fats and oils. First off, your body makes its own fats form the intake of excess calories. Also other fat are gotten from our meals; these are called dietary fats Dietary.

The potentially helpful types of dietary fat are primarily unsaturated fats and they are mostly plant based but can also be found in very few animal sources:

Monounsaturated fatty acids. This type of fat is found in a variety of foods and oils. Research have shown that eating food substances rich in monosaturated fats, helps in the reduction of triglcerides, Low density lipoproteins (LDP) or bad cholesterol and improves the production of High density lipoproteins (HDL) in the blood; this of course in turn can reduce the risk of heart diseases, and type 2 diabetes mellitus.

Polyunsaturated fatty acids. Almost like the monounsaturated fats, this type of fat is found mostly in plant-based foods and oils. Evidence shows that eating foods rich in polyunsaturated fatty acids instead of saturated fats improves blood cholesterol levels by increasing the production of High density lipoproteins and reducing the production of Low density lipoproteins in the blood – this can decrease the chances of having heart disease and may also help decrease the risk of type 2 diabetes mellitus.

Omega-3 fatty acids. One type of polyunsaturated fat is made up of mainly omega-3 fatty acids and may be especially beneficial for heart health. Omega-3, found in some types of fatty fish, and Brazilian nuts they are so good for the heart; they appears to decrease the risk of coronary artery disease. There are many more plant sources of omega-3 fatty acids – However, it has not yet been proven as to whether they can take the place of fish oil in the supply of omega 3 fatty acids. Foods made up mostly of monounsaturated and polyunsaturated fats are liquid at room temperature, such as canola oil, olive oil, safflower oil, peanut oil, sunflower oil and corn oil.

So the way forward here would be to avoid saturated fat and Trans fats which are mostly found in red meat, poultry and full fat dairy products and replace them with monounsaturated or polyunsaturated fats.

CHAPTER 4: HOW TO MAKE THE TRANSITION FROM AN ANIMAL-BASED DIET TO A PLANT-BASED DIET, ONE STEP AT A TIME

Making the transition from an animal-based diet to a plant-based one is not as easy as you would envisage. It is true that plant-based eating became quite well-known in 2018 and has since garnered attention from the public. However, it is important that before you jump on the bandwagon, you should keep in mind that beginning a new diet is one of the most difficult things you may have to do.

If you have been neck-deep into animal-based diets, making the switch to a plant-based one may look like a feat that cant be achieved. You are probably wondering what else is there to eat if you are going to pass up on the dairy, meat and egg, but dont worry, you wont be the first to think that way. You will be shocked to find that there is actually a wide range of choices outside meat, dairy and egg. Not only is there an unlimited option, these meals are delicious and nourishing, and dont have to be so different from what youre already used to.

It will require a ton of discipline, effort, willpower and detailed planning. Plus, it is a terrible idea to jump from meat one day to veggies the next day (you will probably even regret it; switching diets is not as easy.)

It could even get confusing and quite frankly, tiring at the beginning; you may even be tempted to give it up. I will start from now to assure you though that you really can do anything you set your mind to. It doesnt matter if you stumble and fumble every now and then, as long as you are willing to do this, youll do it!

Now, I am going to hold your hands and walk you through every step of the process involved in making the big transition. Be sure to follow every step as a skipped one might make it a lot more difficult for you. Try not to go for short cuts, remember that were trying to do this in a slow and steady way that does not upset your entire body system, especially your gut because of the sudden change from what its used to. It is because of your health that you will need to religiously follow the steps one after the other to safely arrive at the desired destination.
Let us get to the steps, shall we?

Step One - Prepare to Make Your Own Food
This is the first and most important step when it comes to making the big switch. There are not usually a lot of vegan restaurants, except you plan to move to an area with a lot of those and enough money to eat vegan at a restaurant all the time. Bottom line is, it is best and easiest to make your own foods as it ensures that you have a variety to choose from and you can add some spice and creativity to your own meals to make them more enjoyable. Plus, it usually does not take as much time and effort to prepare plant-based meals.
To help, you could find cookbooks with vegan ideas. You could also find ideas and recipes for delicious plant-based meals online; search plant-based diet sites, Instagram, Pinterest and stay creative.

Step Two - Work on a Meal Plan

If your transition is going to be smooth, then you will have to be a little more deliberate with your meal plans. Since you would not be able to down just anything anymore, it is important to have a weekly detailed plan. This will save you energy, time and money. So, I advise that you sit to make your meal plan for the week on Saturdays, so that you have a list of required groceries and time to go shopping for them. As with every other thing, preparation and planning are key ingredients for the success of your transition to plant-based meals.

Step Three - Stock Your Kitchen Up with Healthy Foods
The reason this is so important is because you do not want to always have a long shopping list and you would not always have enough time or money to go shopping. Stocking up will save time and help you make foods without having to go shopping first. It will also help you make foods in a breeze. There are lots of healthier options to shop for at the grocery store like dairy-free milk and tofu. Dont worry about your budget; you will always find healthy alternatives that fit into your budget. You can spend time doing a survey of what is available at the fresh produce and vegetarian aisles.
You will also find a variety of snack options that you can stock up with too, for when you desperately need a snack.

Step Four - Start Slow with Familiar Foods
There are already plant-based meals that you enjoy like oatmeal, potatoes, bean, rice, lentil stew, and pasta, to mention a few. Start with those meals and begin to build on them slowly. Eventually, you will come to realize that there is actually a lot to eat outside meat, eggs and fish. Gradually, you will start to get used to this habit. Remember, there is no pressure. I am not saying you should totally cut off your animal-based diet; note how I used the word "slowly"? These things should not be rushed.
Simply identify what foods are plant-based and slowly start to pay more attention to them.

Step Five - It is Time to cut down a Bit on Your Meat and Processed Food Intake

Now it is time to cut back on your processed food and meat intake. It is not advisable to completely stop taking stuff you are already used to all of a sudden, so I say you start by reducing how much of these you are taking.

This will help your mind; your body and your guts adjust to the newness of it all. You could maybe add salads or fruits and cut down a little on those dairy or meat products you didnt have a thing for anyway. It is easier to start with this and gradually keep replacing animal-based diets with plant-based ones, keeping your favorite recipes and making them plant-based.

For example, if you enjoy eating tacos, you can go for a similar but plant-based alternative like Quinoa Taco.

At this stage, you can skip meat just once a week. You can make "Meatless Mondays" a thing for you considering it is already quite popular. Do not worry if you still eat dairy, eggs and fish. Simply skip meat once a week and keep trying out alternative plant-based diets. What you are doing is that you are gradually shifting your focus.

At this stage, you might also want to keep reading up about plant-based diets and beneficial they are for your health. There are a couple of podcasts to lay your hand on while you are on this journey too.

You could learn about animal welfare and plant-based athletes.

Step Six - Commit to Having Nothing Less than One Plant-Based Meal Everyday

At this stage, you know what it is like to eat more of plant-based meals, so it is time to eat at least one plant-based meal every day, it could be for breakfast, lunch or dinner. You can stick with doing this for breakfast every day. For instance, you can switch from having scrambled eggs for breakfast to having pancakes, or maybe simply add some veggies to the mix. After sometime eating plant-based breakfast, you could start experimenting with lunch and then dinner.

Here are a few breakfast ideas you could try out;

Smoothie bowls, Smoothies

Waffles, French toast

Oatmeal

Chia pudding

Cookies, muffins

Burrito bowls, burrito, tostadas, tacos

Chickpea omelettes, quiches, tofu scrambles

Peanut butter, Avocado toast, Almond butter

Skillets, hash and casseroles with lots of veggies

Salads

Sliced fruit, fruit bowls, sauerkraut, avocado, chopped veggies, hummus.

Coconut or eggplant, tempeh, tofu. Tofu can be dry-fried or baked. You can go for the dry-fry method when you have run out of baked tofu. The dry-fried tofu is crispy and just as yummy. You can also crisp your tempeh in an oven or a pan. To do so, first marinate in garlic powder, maple syrup and soy sauce. This will help if you want a bacon flavor;

Buddha bowls

Vegan cereals

Granola (homemade)

Baked potatoes, with yoghurt, peanut butter, avocado, greens and beans

Berries, yoghurt (should be dairy-free), granola

Fruit salad with almond milk or yoghurt

Hummus and chopped veggies like celery, bell pepper, broccoli and carrot

Just fresh fruit like mangoes, berries, grapes, apples, pineapple, melon, papaya and kiwi

You can have a few healthy nuts that are good for your heart. E.g. cashew, walnuts, almonds. These are a great source of healthy fat.

Fermented sauerkraut is good for your digestion and is similar in function to yoghurt. Another good source of probiotics is kombucha. You can have any of this with breakfast.

Roasted veggies like potatoes, red pepper or roasted onions will come through an amazing taste.

Make some protein pudding using a mixture of pumpkin, water or yoghurt with protein powder.

Sautéed mushrooms are highly delicious and incredibly filling.

You can always add some beans to breakfast, they are also filling and are great alternative sources of protein. You could go for black beans, refried homemade beans.

Avocado is one of the most nutritious fruits ever. It contains healthy fat and lots of fibre to make sure you stay full for a longer period. You can top yours with lemon, sea salt and pepper.

Steamed green vegetables like spinach is a great way to boost your nutrient intake for the day.

All of these breakfast ideas are definitely fun ways to enjoy a good breakfast, you would not even grumble about how "boring" you think plant-based meals are, because they are in fact, very far from boring.

What is so great about these meals is how quickly you can fix them up. Of course, this does not mean all plant-based meals are quick fixes, you can have an elaborate meal if you want to but I am showing you simple ideas for lazy days and breakfast, when you are leaving home for work.

By eating at least one plant-based meal every single day, you will be consuming enough healthy nutrients and fibre; your guts will need it so it gradually gets used to the change. Plus, as you eat plant-based meals more, you are less likely to be as dependent on animal-based meals as you used to be. You will also gradually learn that you can do without processed foods.

Remember that you will also have to make a few tweaks to your meal plans since you will now be having plant-based meals more often. It is a good thing you are already learning to stock up on healthy foods, right? You will need it now more than before. You will also have to learn new recipes and be ready to try out new stuff.

Stick with this stage for about a month before moving on to the next one.

Step Seven - Watch the Protein Intake

Typically, the body needs about a gram per kilogram of our weight on an average. People, however, sometimes take way beyond what is required because they want to get as much as possible. While we are talking about your transitioning, it would not hurt for me to mention that more is not always better, no matter how good a thing supposedly is. Consuming excessive amounts of protein can become harmful. Technically, it is not that we need to consume so much protein; it is that we meet all nine essential amino acid requirements. Our body is unable to produce these essential amino acids on its own; this is why it is an essential nutritional requirement.

The good news is that every plant food has these amino acids, even though in different quantities. The point though is that eating plant-based diets can easily supply the required protein, and you do not even have to consume so much protein. You would not be deficient in protein as long as you are eating plant-based meals along with calories and whole foods.

Step Eight: - Reduce Your Consumption of Meat to Only Once a Week

At this point, plant-based meals are almost becoming a way of life, so it is time to cut down your meat consumption even further till you are only eating it once a week. Do not rush this stage, you will have to remain here for another one or two months to get used to eating meat just once a week. It can be excruciating at first, but since you are already getting used to plant-based meals, you may soon not even notice that you are eating meat only once a week. You can go further to cutting it down to once in a few weeks or even once a month.

You can replace your beloved meat recipes with these ones while you work your way through it all;

Use jackfruit for pulled pork

Replace beef with cauliflower rice in stuff like chili

Replace beef burgers with yummy veggie burgers

For burger patties or fajitas, use mushrooms (portobello)

In place of beef, use lentils or walnuts for taco meat

For bacon, go with coconut, eggplant or tofu

In place of meat sausages, go for vegan sausages

Substitute tofu, seitan or tempeh for meat

Step Nine: - Completely Take out Meat from Your Diet

It is finally the adult step! Stay a bit on the previous step before moving over here, especially if you do not think you are ready. Remember you are doing this at your pace and the last thing you want is to be pressured into this. So, take your time.

Once you are certain you are ready for this step, then congratulations!

Since you should now be familiar with preparing plant-based meals, you will have very little problem adjusting to the no-meat rule.

It will probably help to go back to why you are taking this journey again. This may be necessary to keep your head in the game. Check back on some of the podcasts or articles you have listened to or read and stay on them again. This way, your reasons are ever on your mind. Constantly do this if you think that you need some motivation to continue. Do not worry; you totally have it under control!

You will also have to reduce or completely eliminate fish from your meals too. Also, try as much as you can to stick with whole foods as processed foods sometimes contain same nutrients with animal products (like lots of amino acids and saturated fats)and they are outright unhealthy. If you are going to take processed foods, do so only once in a while. Educate yourself concerning nutrition and learn new recipes. If all of this is too much, there are plant-based dietitians that could help you through the transitioning and help you settle comfortably into your new lifestyle.

Step Ten - Reduce Your Dairy Intake

I know how difficult it can be trying to cut dairy off of your meals. But it gets easier as you get used to it overtime. To make it easier, I will show you a step-by-step way to cutting down on your dairy intake gradually.

Start with the Cows Milk

It is easiest to start the reduction from milk. Lucky for you, animal-based milk is not the only kind in the market. A lot of plant-based milk products exist and you can even make yours. It is easy to replace the dairy milk with dairy-free ones, so start with that.

Next up, Yoghurt

Once you have successfully taken dairy-free milk for a few weeks, the next step to cutting dairy products is yoghurt. You can learn to make your own yoghurt at home using almond, coconut or cashew. If you cant spare sometime to get this done or you cant seem to get it, then there are also alternatives at the store like Yoso.

Then Cheese

This is probably the hard part for a lot of people because it seems impossible to find a befitting alternative for how gloriously cheese melts. Before you start sulking and thinking about giving up, remember how far youve come, you dont want to throw all of that away.
Truth is, you will eventually come to terms with not eating cheese. Plus, you can still get vegan cheese at the store or make yours if youre ready for some fun and adventure!

The Dairy Extras come next

Examples of dairy extras include whipped cream, sour cream, cheese sauce, and cream. All of these can easily be replaced vegan alternatives or you also learn to make them yourself at home making use of ingredients like cashew, coconut milk, soft tofu. The best part about the homemade versions is that you can be creative and add your own twist to them.
While you are at the dairy stage, be sure to experiment with a lot of alternatives and find one that works for you. Alternatives to try include tofu, cashews with vegan sour cream, cashew or almond, yeast, vegan coffee creamer, try tofu ricotta. In place of mayonnaise, do avocado or vegan mayo or go for vegan cheese at a grocery store if you want some nachos or pizza.

Step Eleven - Reduce Your Egg Intake

Eggs are a huge part of peoples meals and again, this is another difficult stage. Many people can almost not do without eggs for breakfast and you are probably one of them. The good news though is that there will always be healthier and more suitable options to go for.

Begin by reducing how much eggs you are eating gradually, while going in search of suitable alternatives. Here are a few alternatives:

Tofu scramble
Burrito with veggie sweet potato
Oats
Sweet potatoes
Avocado toast
Breakfast burritos
Chia pudding
Breakfast bowl, chipotle sauce
Toast with jam and almond butter
Breakfast bowl (grain free)
Smoothie with avocado and chocolate, or pumpkin and peanut butter

Altering your recipe bit to find an alternative of egg for your baking is another way to cut down on the eggs. You can replace the egg with banana, fibre, flax eggs, soft tofu, psyllium fibre, applesauce, chia eggs, etc.

Step Twelve - Completely Eliminate Eggs from Your Meals

This is the final step. If you have gotten here, then kudos! You have done an amazing job and I hope this journey has been an exciting one for you. At this stage, it is time to completely take eggs out of your diet. It should not take so much effort considering you have already cut some of your most cherished meals off, including meat, fish and dairy products. You have also been doing lots of experimenting finding what works for you as a vegan alternative for eggs. So, you are already almost all plant-based. What is left is taking the egg out completely after finding great and interesting alternatives.

It is important that your meals are interesting, creative and fun. Do not go all bougie if you know you do not have to, or if your kitchen skills are like Thomas Edisons singing skills. Stick with recipes that you are used to already and simply go for vegan alternatives for ingredients. This way, you are not tempted to go back.

You may have to learn ways to make your old recipes much more fun. If you get tired of eating the same old salad, then find new salad recipes or find creative ways to enjoy veggies. Do not be so rigid too, so when you have a craving for dessert, do not hesitate to treat yourself to a nice plant-based treat.

Something that will help you is your company. Like-minded people will keep you motivated and learning new stuff. You can find these people on social media. Find books, podcasts, movies, anything. As time progresses, you will truly start to enjoy and crave these meals, and youll notice that indeed you feel so much better.

What You Should Do at Events and Holidays

Make no mistake; your new diet choice will make things a bit difficult for you and your relationships, friendships or family, because of the predominance of animal-based eating. It could be confusing and quite frankly, frustrating, attending a social event with animal-based meals and there is nothing for you because you are strictly eating plant-based meals. So, I now I do not have to but I will just show you a few ways to handle this. Thank me later!

Try to focus less on the food and focus more on the fact that you are able to be at the event to maybe support a dear friend or family member. If it is a family gathering, do some gratitude check and fix your mind on how you are grateful to be spending time with family.

Do not let anyone make you feel that you are simply being unnecessary just because they do not get your choices. No one should make you feel bad about your dietary choices.

If there is tea or water served at the event, and then help yourself to some.

If you know that expecting plant-based meals at the event you are attending is like expecting an ape to speak Chinese, then spend some time to make your own delicious vegan food and share with your friends at the event. Who knows, you just might be able to convince someone that quitting animal-based meal is not so bad after all. You dont have to cook up something fancy, except youre up for it. But a little appetizer or dessert will do.

In a situation where you are not sure what food options will be made available at the event, it is best to confirm with the host or ask if you can bring a dish to help.

Get some snacks that are animal-free. It could be nuts, hummus, veggies, and chips. Even guacamole is a good snack option too. This way, you are munching something while others are too at an event.

The need to fit in might hit you in large, almost uncontrollable waves, but do not let your feelings get in the way of your choices or decisions. In order to get comfortable being the odd one out, you can make jokes about it. If people ask why you are doing what you are doing, do not hesitate to fill them in and explain with patience, making sure that you do not come off as haughty or condescending. If nobody seems interested, then there is no need to talk about it, just move on. You will eventually get used to it.

Keep your reason on your mind. This will remind you of the reason you started the journey in the first place.

If you have no time to prepare anything, and you are not familiar enough with the host, then it is best for you to eat a huge meal before leaving the house, unless it is a dinner party you are attending. With a full tummy, you will most likely not even bother with whats being served at the dessert table. This is probably the biggest life saver of all the points.

Through all of this, remember that transitioning takes time and you will rely on trial and error most of the time until you find what exactly rocks your boat. I am saying this to say that you should take it easy with yourself and not be too hard. Simply find your rhythm and flow with it.

Healthy Habits to Support your Transitioning

Apart from our food, health involves so many other things like exercise and stress management. Now that your eating habits are coming together, it is a good time to incorporate some healthy habits to your routine to keep your overall self healthy.

Here are a few things you should do for improved health as you eat right:

Drink water, lots of it. While you are getting nourished, you do not want to get dehydrated. First thing in the morning you should do is gulp down a large glass of water, then keep drinking enough water throughout the day.

Carry out a lot of physical activities either in form of work out sessions or otherwise. This will leave you feeling and looking great. This will also leave you sleeping better. I am not saying you should dwell at the gym more than half your life; all I am saying is that you should try to break a sweat and be physically active.

Meditation will help calm your head and has been shown to be useful to your health.

Spend at least thirty minutes to read every day. Time spent reading cant be time wasted. Plus, reading improves your life.

Take some to sit with nature. This is a healthy way to manage stress and detox your mind.

Try to sleep better. Your body will be grateful for it.

Keep a journal as it will help reduce stress and anxiety. It will also help keep your focus alive and cause you to have a strengthened vision for your life. Its also generally just a good way to relax.

Establishing beautiful connections with humans plays a big role in longevity and happiness. Studies show that people who are surrounded by loving relationships tend to live more and are generally happier compared with lonely people.

CHAPTER 5: RECEPIES OF PLANT BASED DIET

SMOOTHIE

Apple and fennel pomegranate smoothie

INGREDIENTS:
2 pomegranates

1 apple
½ fennel
1 teaspoon lemon juice
2 cm fresh ginger

PREPARETION:
Cut the pomegranates in half and squeeze them with a juicer (alternatively shell them and keep the seeds eliminating the bitter white part). Keep the juice aside.
Peel the apples, remove the stalk, the core and the seeds, then cut them into four
Wash the fennel and remove the woody parts and the stem. Cut it into slices lengthwise.
Squeeze half a lemon and filter the juice necessary to eliminate the seeds. Peel the ginger with a sharp knife.
Put the pomegranate juice (or the seeds), the apples and the fennel in the centrifuge, operating it at medium speed and adding the ginger, half a glass of water and the previously prepared lemon juice to the mixture. Strain the juice obtained.

Cucumber, green apple and ginger smoothie

INGREDIENTS:
1 cucumber
1 green apple
3cm ginger
1 teaspoon of honey

PREPARATION:
Peel the cucumber and cut it into slices.
Clean the ginger by removing it from its bark
Everything is put in a blender and mixed until puree is obtained.
You can sweeten it a little, given the acidity of the green apple, with a teaspoon of acacia honey.

Carrots and tangerins smoothie

INGREDIENTS:
Carrots (250 gr)
Tangerines (55 gr)
Pumpkin seeds (2 tablespoons)
Banana (1)
Ginger (half a spoon)

Water (230 ml)

PREPARATION:
Chop the carrots, peel the tangerines and the banana, and grate the ginger. Put everything in the blender until a velvety and creamy consistency is reached. If necessary, add water to make it more liquid.

Avocado, spinach, banana and chia seeds smoothie

INGREDIENTS:
1 ripe avocado (about 100 grams, without peel and seed)
1 ripe banana (about 100 grams, without peel)
50 gr of spinach
1 tablespoon of chia seeds
1 tablespoon of lemon juice
100 ml of rice milk

PREPARATION:
Prepare all the ingredients: wash the spinach and drain well; wash the avocado, peel it, remove the inner seed and cut it into small pieces; peel the banana and cut it into small pieces. Pour the spinach, avocado and banana pieces into the blender, then add the lemon juice, chia seeds and rice milk. Check the result and add more rice milk if the smoothie seems too solid, then blend again for a few seconds.
Pour the smoothie obtained in two glasses or 2 glass bottles and garnish with two straws.

Apple and cinnamon smoothie

INGREDIENTS:

2 Apples (about 300 gr without core and peel)
1 tablespoon of lemon juice
200 ml of millet milk
1 teaspoon of cinnamon

PREPARATION:
First wash the apples, peel them and remove the core
Cut the apples into small pieces and place them in the blender with the millet milk and lemon juice, which is used to keep the apple from blackening
Take the blender until foamed and finally add the cinnamon powder
Pour into 2 glasses and enjoy with a straw.

Pumpkin smoothie with oat flakes, cinnamon and star anise

INGREDIENTS:
200 g of clean Pumpkin (already stripped of peel and seeds)
1 large orange
20 g of oat flakes
A pinch of cinnamon powder
A pinch of star anise powder
Cinnamon stick (to decorate)
Star anise (to decorate)

PREPARATION:
First place the oat flakes in a hot pan and toast them for 5 minutes, turning them continuously so as not to burn them. Meanwhile, the oat flakes cool down, dry the pumpkin and cut it into pieces of about 2 cm. When they are cold, chop the oat flakes in the blender and set them aside.

Place the pumpkin, the juice of an orange, a pinch of cinnamon powder and one of star anise powder in the blender and blend until smooth. If necessary, add water until the desired consistency is obtained.
Pour the mixture into a glass and garnish with the chopped oat flakes, a cinnamon stick and a piece of star anise.

This smoothie is based on pumpkin, therefore ideal to prepare in the fall, when this vegetable is in season, providing us with all the nutrients needed to face the winter. Pumpkin is in fact rich in beta-carotene, a precious antioxidant, fiber and mineral salts such as magnesium, useful for the nervous system, and potassium, which counteracts water retention.

Chocolate smoothie with chia and banana seeds

INGREDIENTS:
1 Banana
2 tablespoons of bitter cocoa
5 dates
3 ice cubes (optional)

30 g of extra-dark chocolate
1 tablespoon of chia seeds
1 tablespoon of grated coconut
140 ml of almond milk

PREPARATION:
First, peel the banana, cut it into chunks and remove the dates from the core.
Put the bananas and dates inside the blender together with the ice (optional), the coconut, the bitter cocoa and the almond milk.
Run the blender until you get a smooth, smooth, smooth smoothie.
Serve the smoothie in a glass and garnish with some extra-thick flaky chocolate and chia seeds. If you want an "eat and drink" smoothie, add a few slices of banana.

Due to its ingredients, in particular dates, coconut and dark chocolate, it is a rather caloric smoothie, ideal for regaining energy in the middle of the morning but to be consumed in moderation, especially for those who are on a diet or in any case attentive to the line.

Blueberry smoothie with oat milk and banana

INGREDIENTS:
2 bananas
250 gr of blueberries
4 ice cubes (optional)
250 ml of oat milk
PREPARATION:
First wash the blueberries carefully. Peel the banana and cut it into small pieces.
Place the fruit, ice and half of the almond milk inside the special container and operate the blender.
Add water or other oat milk to taste, until you reach the consistency you want for your smoothie.
Serve the blueberry smoothie with oat milk and banana in a glass , garnishing it, if necessary, with banana and fresh blueberries.

Peach smoothie with almond milk and fresh mint

INGREDIENTS:
2 ripe peaches
150 ml of almond milk
80 gr of white soy yogurt
6 leaves of fresh mint
3 ice cubes

PREPARATION:
Wash the peaches thoroughly under running water. Peel them and remove them from the core. Then roughly cut them into pieces. Clean the mint leaves with a wet sponge.
Pour the peaches cut into pieces, almond milk, white yogurt, ice and 4 mint leaves into the blender.

Turn on the blender and leave it running until you have a smooth and full-bodied smoothie.
Serve the smoothie in a glass with a decorative mint leaf.

Antioxidant smoothie with watermelon and grapes

INGREDIENTS:
250 gr of watermelon (weight without peel)
200 gr of black grapes, with or without seeds
2 spoons of fresh lime juice

PREPARATION:
Cut the watermelon into slices and put it in the blender, then wash the grapes and cut the berries in half, also removing the seeds.
Add the grapes in the blender together with the lime juice and a pinch of salt and blend for at least 30 seconds, until you have reached a creamy consistency.
If it is too dry, add a few more drops of lime juice. Now your smoothie is ready!

Frozen smoothies with ginger and peanut butter

INGREDIENTS:
3 Ripe bananas
1 piece of fresh Ginger root (about 4/5 cm)
75 ml of unsweetened almond milk
1 tablespoon agave syrup
1 tablespoon lemon juice
2 teaspoons organic peanut butter

PREPARATION:

For this recipe choose rather ripe and soft bananas. Peel the bananas, cut them into small pieces and sprinkle them with lemon juice to prevent them from turning black.

Peel the ginger and cut it into thin slices, then transfer all the ingredients into the blender glass and operate intermittently until a soft and creamy consistency is obtained.

Wet a popsicle mold and pour the smoothie, insert some toothpicks.

Place the mold in the freezer for 6/7 hours, preferably for an entire night, to allow the smoothies to solidify.

Before using them, immerse the mold for a few seconds in warm water to extract frozen smoothies more easily.

Apple, pear and cinnamon smoothie

INGREDIENTS:
Apples 470 g
Ice 170 g
Soy milk 250 g
Cinnamon powder 2 g
Pears 260 g
Honey 50 g

PREPARATION:
Wash the apple and cut them in half , then divide them into wedges, deprive them of the internal seeds and peel them.
Then cut each wedge into slices and then into cubes .
At this point take care of the pears: wash them, cut them into wedges , deprive them of the internal seeds , peel them and reduce them to cubes of the same size as the apples.
Pour the ice into the glass of a mixer , add the apples and the pears
Add the honey , the cinnamon and finally the milk
Blend everything until a homogeneous mixture , then transfer it to the glasses .

Decorate your Apple, pear and cinnamon Smoothie according to your tastes and serve cold .

Mimosa smoothie

INGREDIENTS:
200 g low-fat yogurt
1 Banana
1 Golden apple
1 Lemon juice
1 Orange juice
100 ml Sparkling wine
100 g crushed ice
2 tsp sugar
1 teaspoon vanilla extract

PREPARATION:
To begin, wash the apple, remove the peel, the core with the seeds and cut it into small pieces.
Then peel and cut the banana and add the pieces of fruit in the blender, along with the lemon and orange juice.
Incorporate also sugar, vanilla extract, yogurt, sparkling wine and ice, then blend at maximum speed.

Pineapple and fresh ginger smoothie

INGREDIENTS:
170 gr diced pineapple
1 teaspoon grated fresh ginger
1 jar of yogurt (light or soy)
230 ml of pineapple juice
1 pinch of ground cinnamon
½ glass of ice

PREPARAION:
Put all the ingredients together in a blender.
Blend at high speed until you get a creamy mixture.
Pour into two glasses and serve immediately.

Soy, banana and peanut butter smoothie

INGREDIENTS:
½ cup of soft tofu (100 g)
1 cup of soy milk (250 ml)
1 cold banana
½ tablespoon of peanut butter (5 g)

PREPARATION:
Blend all the ingredients for a few seconds till you get a homogeneous drink

Protein smoothie with oats, banana and barley

INGREDIENTS:
15 g of oat flakes
250 ml of water
100 g of banana pulp
5 g of soluble barley
20 g of concentrated soy protein

PREPARATION:
Prepare the oat milk: soften the oat flakes in the water for at least half an hour. Blend the flakes with the water, then filter through a cloth to separate the spent pulp from the liquid part.
Collect the oat milk again in the blender glass, then add the banana (peeled and cut into slices), the soy protein and two teaspoons of soluble barley. Blend everything until a smooth and velvety mixture is obtained. For a more diluted drink, we recommend adding a little water.
Consume the protein shake immediately or in any case within half an hour of preparation.

Persimmon and pear smoothie

INGREDIENTS:
200 g of persimmons
200 g of pears
1 piece of ginger
Juice and zest of 400 g (2 medium) of untreated oranges

PREPARATION:
Gently wash the fruit: peel the persimmon and collect the pulp in the glass blender. Dice the pear (if organic, you can keep the peel) and add it to the blender. Flavor with orange zest and grated ginger.
Cut the oranges in half and squeeze the juice.
Add the orange juice to the other ingredients.
Blend for a couple of minutes, until you get the right consistency. If desired, add ice cubes.
To fully appreciate the active ingredients, immediately consume the smoothie. If desired, add a teaspoon of bitter cocoa.

> Persimmon smoothie the intestine is a food belonging to the group of sweets.
> It has a low energy intake, mainly provided by carbohydrates, followed by proteins and only by traces of lipids.
> Carbohydrates are mainly simple, low biological value

> peptides and unsaturated fatty acids.
> It contains a high dose of fiber and cholesterol is absent.
> It does not provide gluten, lactose and histamine.

Protein smoothie with almonds, banana and cocoa

INGREDIENTS:
100 g of banana
5 g (1 teaspoon) of bitter cocoa
80 g (5-6 cubes) of ice
300 ml of soy milk
20 g of almonds
30 g of concentrated soy protein
PREPARATION:
Toast the almonds on a very hot pan, taking care not to burn the surface.
Pour the almonds into the glass of the electric blender. Add the peeled and sliced banana, the bitter cocoa powder, the soy milk and the protein powders.
Blend all the ingredients, adding the ice (5-6 cubes): 2 minutes are enough to make the ice mince / melt and to obtain a smoothie with the right consistency.
Pour into glasses and serve.
The protein shake can be kept in the refrigerator for a few days, tightly closed in a glass jar or in a bottle.

Raw strawberry smoothie with hemp seed milk

INGREDIENTS:
100 g of banana
250 g of strawberries
200 ml of hemp seed milk
15 g stevia
Untreated lemon juice
Optional: a few mint leaves
PREPARATION:
Wash the strawberries, dry them gently, then remove the stalk and cut them into pieces.
Peel the banana, cut it into slices and combine the slices in the blender, together with the strawberries, stevia, lemon juice and flavor with a few mint leaves. Pour the hemp seed milk and whisk until a thick drink is obtained.
Add a few ice cubes to taste and consume immediately.

Anti-cellulite smoothie

INGREDIENTS:
150 g of blueberries
150 g of pineapple
200 g of pink grapefruit
150 g of strawberries
100 g of raspberries
A few ice cubes

PREPARATION:
Clean and cut the pineapple
Wash the blueberries and raspberries and dry them gently.
Wash the strawberries, dry them and remove the stalk.
Cut the pink grapefruit and remove the albedo, the amarotic white film.

Gather all the fruit in the blender glass, along with a few ice cubes (important to prevent overheating of the active ingredients).

To fully benefit from the properties of the active ingredients, it is recommended to consume the anti-cellulite smoothie immediately.

Mango Ginger-Cashew Smoothie

INGREDIENTS:
1 heaping cup frozen mango chunks
5 whole cashews
1/2 teaspoon grated fresh ginger (or 1/8 teaspoon dry ground ginger)
1/2 cup almond milk
1/2 teaspoon honey, optional
2-3 ice cubes

PREPARATION:
Place all ingredients in the high-speed blender and puree until thick and frothy.

Creamy Zucchini Blueberry Smoothie

INGREDIENTS:
1 large ripe banana (previously peeled, sliced, and frozen)
1 cup frozen wild blueberries (organic when possible)
1 large stem celery
2/3 cup sliced zucchini (fresh or frozen)
1 handful greens (spinach is best // organic when possible)
1 Tbsp hemp seeds (or sub vegan protein powder)
1/4 tsp ground cinnamon
1 cup light coconut milk (or store-bought // or sub water)

1/2 tsp maca powder

PREPARATION:
Add all ingredients to a high-speed blender and blend on high until creamy and smooth. Taste and adjust flavor as needed, adding more cinnamon for warmth/spice, banana for sweetness, or zucchini for creaminess.
Divide between 2 serving glasses (or more or less if altering batch size) and garnish with blueberries and hemp seeds (optional). Best when fresh. Store leftovers covered in the refrigerator.

Blueberry banana almond butter smoothie

INGREDIENTS:
1 1/2 cups cold almond milk
1 cup fresh or frozen blueberries
1 medium fresh or frozen ripe banana
3 tablespoons smooth almond butter
1 to 2 tablespoons honey
1 tablespoon raw flax seeds optional
1 cup ice optional.
PREPARATION:
Combine all ingredients in a blender and process until smooth and thoroughly blended, about 30 seconds to 1 minute. Serve.

Kiwi and avocado smoothie

INGREDIENTS:
3 kiwis, peeled and roughly chopped
1 ripe avocado, peeled, pitted and chopped
½ cup packed fresh spinach
1 cup coconut milk
2 cups peach juice
2 tablespoons honey
1 teaspoon grated fresh ginger
5 ice cubes

PREPARATION:
Add avocado, spinach, coconut milk, peach juice, honey, ginger and ice to a blender. Purée until smooth.
Add kiwi and pulse just until blended. Divide amongst 4 glasses.
Garnish glasses with kiwi slices if desired.

Chocolate, banana and almond smoothie

INGREDIENTS:
2 bananas (medium, peeled, sliced, and frozen)
2 tablespoons almond butter
1 cup Silk Unsweetened Vanilla Almond Milk
1 tablespoon chia seeds
1 1/2 tablespoons unsweetened cocoa powder
1/2 cup ice

PREPARATION:
Place the bananas (reserve 4 slices to garnish prepared smoothie), almond butter, Silk Unsweetened Vanilla Almond Milk, chia seeds, cocoa powder, and ice in the jar of a blender.

Puree ingredients on high speed, or on the "smoothie" setting (if available), until completely smooth.

Divide mixture between 4 cups or glasses.

If desired, garnish the top of each cup with Mini Chocolate Chips, Sliced Almonds, and Sliced Bananas for a nice presentation.

Serve immediately with a spoon.

VELOUTE & SOUP

Potato soup with Saffron

INGREDIENTS:
5 medium potatoes
1 carrot
1 shallot
2 sachets of saffron
150 dl of vegetable broth`
chives
vegan butter
salt and pepper.

PREPARATION:
To prepare the saffron potato soup, peel the potatoes and carrot and cut them into cubes. Also peel the shallot and finely chop it. Brown it in a saucepan with a knob of vegan butter. Add the vegetables and cook by mixing. Cover everything with hot broth and bring to a boil. Let it go over medium heat until the vegetables are tender.
Collect the vegetables in the bowl of a food processor. Correct with salt and pepper. Add a little broth in which you will have melted the saffron and blend. Continue incorporating more broth until you get the consistency of a velvety.
Spread the cream into four holsters.

Cream of pumpkin and potato soup with mushrooms

INGREDIENTS:
1 kg pumpkin
200 g potatoes
1 small white onion
1 liter of vegetable broth
150 g homemade bread
100 g poplar mushrooms
thyme
125 ml of low-fat white yogurt
smoked paprika
30 g sliced almonds
pepper
salt
oil

PREPARATION:
To prepare the Pumpkin and Potato Cream Soup with Mushrooms, cut the pumpkin and potatoes into cubes. Peel the onion and cut it into pieces. Heat two tablespoons of oil in a saucepan, add the onion and let it simmer on low heat for a few minutes. Add the pumpkin and potatoes and season with salt and pepper. Stir and pour a part of the broth until the vegetables are covered. Cook over medium heat, adding the remaining broth, for about 30 minutes, until the vegetables are tender.
In the meantime, in a non-stick pan, cook the mushrooms with a spoonful of oil and a sprig of thyme for about 15 minutes. Season with salt and pepper.

To prepare the croutons, cut the bread into cubes of about 2 centimetres, arrange them on a baking tray lined with parchment paper and season with a drizzle of oil. Brown the croutons of bread in a preheated oven at 200° for about 5 minutes.

Once the velvety cooking is complete, blend it with an immersion mixer to obtain a creamy consistency.

Flavour the white yogurt with smoked paprika. Serve the velvety hot, accompanied by the flavored cream, the mushrooms, the sliced almonds, the bread croutons and some fresh thyme leaves.

Potato and avocado cream

INGREDIENTS:
6 medium potatoes
100 g of low-fat or vegan cheese
2 avocados
1 l of rice milk
salt
black pepper
parsley for garnish

PREPARATION:
To prepare the potato and avocado cream, boil the potatoes in their skins, taking about 40 minutes from the boil. Peel them and pass them to the potato masher when they are still hot.

In a bowl, cream the cheese with the help of a whisk. Dilute the mixture by adding the warm milk a little at a time.

Transfer to a pot and add the mashed potatoes little by little, mixing well to mix them with the liquid without lumps forming. Alternatively, and to obtain a finer result, you can combine the two compounds and then blend everything with an immersion blender. Season with salt and freshly ground pepper and thicken over low heat, so that the cream never reaches a boil. In the meantime, peel the avocados, cut them into small pieces and distribute them on the bottom of a serving dish. When the cream is ready pour it on the plate to completely cover the avocados. Garnish the potato and avocado cream with a few slices of the fruit, a flake of cheese, parsley leaves, pepper and serve immediately.

Cream of asparagus soup with potato balls

INGREDIENTS:
600 g di asparagi
2 patate
1 cipolla
brodo vegetale
1 cucchiaio raso di farina
extra virgin olive oil
4 tablespoons of low-fat cream
2-3 tablespoons of sesame seeds
low-fat cheese

salt

PREPARATION:
Remove 2 centimeters of the hard part of the asparagus stalks, peel them with a potato peeler, wash them and cut them into small pieces. Peel and finely chop the onion, peel, wash and dice a potato.
Heat 4 tablespoons of oil in a saucepan and sauté the vegetables over a moderate heat for a few minutes, sprinkle with flour, cook for a few moments, sprinkle with 6 decilitres of hot broth and continue cooking for 20 minutes.
Pass the soup with an immersion blender until it is smooth and creamy.
To make the meatballs, peel the other potato, wash it, cut it into pieces and steam it for about 20 minutes. Pass it in the potato masher, season it with salt and 2 tablespoons of low-fat cheese.
With wet hands modeled balls as big as hazelnuts and roll them in the sesame seeds, pressing them lightly so that they stick. Divide the velvety into 4 dishes, garnish each portion with a spoonful of lean cream,
and some meatballs

Cream of carrot, ginger and spiced chickpeas

INGREDIENTS:
FOR THE VELVETY
1 kg of carrots
4 cm of fresh ginger
1 clove of garlic
1 small yellow onion
1/4 teaspoon turmeric
1/4 teaspoon cinnamon
1/4 teaspoon pimenton (or paprika)

hot vegetable broth
extra virgin olive oil
salt
pepper
FOR THE CHICKPEAS
150 g of chickpeas already cooked
cumin
pimenton (or paprika)
extra virgin olive oil
salt
pepper
TO SERVE
sour cream to taste
parsley (or coriander)

PREPARATION:
Prepare all the ingredients. Peel the carrots by removing the ends, peel them and reduce them to not too thick slices.
Finely chop the onion and let it stew gently in a saucepan together with olive oil, grated ginger and crushed garlic clove. Add the spices (turmeric, cinnamon and pimenton), cook for 30 seconds and add the carrot slices
Cover with the vegetable broth and cook until the carrots are tender enough to be blended. Reduce everything in a homogeneous cream with an immersion blender, adding more hot broth if necessary to adjust the consistency. Season with salt and pepper. While the velvety is cooking, collect the well-drained chickpeas in a bowl and season them with oil, salt, pepper and spices.
Transfer them to a baking tray lined with parchment paper and cook them under the grill at maximum power, turning them often, until they have just become crispy. Spread the carrot cream on the serving dishes, complement it with sour cream to taste, chopped parsley and spiced chickpeas. Serve immediately.

Cream of cauliflower and coconut milk

INGREDIENTS:
400 g of steamed cauliflower
150 g coconut milk
1/2 glass of water
1/2 teaspoon of turmeric powder
salt
pepper
fresh grated ginger
PREPARATION:
Steam the cauliflower and use 400 grams for the velvety sauce. With an immersion mixer, reduce the cauliflower to cream by adding the coconut milk, salt and pepper.
Pass the cream through a strainer to obtain a more silky texture. Cook over low heat for a few minutes and for greater fluidity add a little cold water. Mix and pour into the serving dishes. Complete with turmeric powder and a grated fresh ginger.

Cream of Romanesco broccoli

INGREDIENTS:
1 broccolo romanesco
olio extravergine di oliva
sale
pepe
8 nocciole tostate

PREPARATION:
Boil the broccoli in lightly salted water for 15 minutes and then drain it while keeping a little cooking water. Remove the green leaves at the base of the broccoli and keep them aside. Cream the broccoli with a dip mixer, adding a drizzle of extra virgin olive oil, salt, pepper and the boiling water. Do the same operation with the green leaves, however pouring only oil, salt and pepper.
In a hot non-stick pan, toast the hazelnuts for 2-3 minutes and then chop them with a knife. Pour the broccoli cream into the serving dishes and complete with the cream of the leaves and a spoonful of chopped hazelnuts.

Part 2

Introduction

Plant-based diet can vary from one person to another. However, the foundational idea is that we try to avoid processed food as much as possible and choose to use what we receive from the beautiful planet that we live in. By that, I mean the incredible ingredients derived from the earth. In essence, plant-based diet comes with a few benefits.

Plant-based diet avoids using processed foods as much as possible.

There are no animal products in the diet.

The categories that are majorly included are vegetables, fruits, seeds and nuts, legumes, whole grains, and herbs and spices.

The diet tries to limit the use of sugar, wheat-flour, and oil as much as possible.

It focuses on the quality of food, mostly utilizing locally or farm-produced organic foods

An important thing to remember here is that there are minimally processed foods included in the plant-based diet, such as non-dairy milk, tofu, and whole-wheat paste, to name a few. Overall, we aim to keep processed foods where they belong: on supermarket shelves, not in our refrigerators.

When people look at the list of foods that come in a plant-based diet, they are often focused on how little we have to work on. However, that is probably due to the fact that many of the meat options have suddenly been removed. It feels as though a major part of the diet has been excluded due to it. How can life be fun without a nice steak? What can we do without chicken wings? Is there anything that can be done without a delicious fish?

In reality, there are numerous ingredients that you can work with. Additionally, the fun is not just in the ingredients but how we prepare them. The growing demand has seen a rise in people trying out new recipes and mashing up ingredients in interesting ways. Have you heard of smoothies that contain cayenne pepper? Sounds pretty exciting, doesnt it? We are going to look at such wonderful and delicious recipes along with so many more dishes that use wholesome and natural ingredients.

People who follow plant-based diets and consume a wide variety of fruits, vegetables and pulses are likely to find it easier to achieve their target of five days.

Some people are doing it; some people are talking about it, but there is still a lot of confusion about what a whole plant-based diet actually entails. Since we split food into their macronutrients: sugars, proteins, and fats, most of us are uncertain about nutrition. What if we were able to put these macronutrients back together again in order to free your mind from confusion and stress? The secret here is simplicity.

Chapter 1: The Basics Of A Plant-Based Diet

What Is A Plant-Based Diet?
Whole foods are foods that come from the earth unprocessed. Now, on a whole food plant-based diet, we eat some minimally processed foods like whole bread, whole wheat pasta, tofu, nondairy milk, and some nuts and seed butter. All of these are fine as long as they are handled to a minimum. So here are the different categories:
Legumes (basically lentils and beans) of whole grains.
Fruits and vegetables
Nuts and seeds (including nut butter)
Herbs and spices
All categories mentioned above constitute an entire diet based on plants. Directions them is where the fun comes in; how to season and cook them; and how to mix and match to give them great flavor and variety in your meals. In this book, there are chapters devoted to plant-based recipes that can give you an idea of what you can easily whip up in your kitchen or the special meals that you can make for your friends. So long, so you regularly eat these foods, you will forever forget about sugars, protein, and fat.
Now, some may say, "Well, I cant eat soy," "I dont like tofu," and so on. Well, the beauty of an entire diet based on food plants is that if you dont like some food, like soy, in this case, you dont have to eat it. In a whole plant-based diet, it is not a necessary component. Instead of barley, you can get brown rice, quinoa instead of wheat; Im sure you catch the drift right now. It really does not matter. Only find the right thing for you.
Just because you decided to adopt a plant-based diet lifestyle, that doesnt mean its a healthy diet. Plant-based diets have a fair share of junk and other unhealthy foods, case and point, regular veggie pizza, and non-dairy ice cream consumption.

Staying healthy requires you to eat healthy foods–even in a dietary setting, based on plants.

A few words that fly around are a similar eating style, but theyre both distinct. That doesnt mean youre going to have to tag yourself to adhere to that way of eating; these words define various ways of eating to help you understand what types of food choices are in a particular class. This analysis can also help you understand how a diet based on a crop blends into the larger picture.

Plant-based: This way of eating is based on berries, vegetables, rice, legumes, nuts, and seeds with few or no foods of animal origin. The plant-based diet is preferably a vegan diet with some versatility in the intermediate stages, with the intention of becoming 100% plant-based over time.

Vegan: It describes someone who eats nothing from an animal, be it fish, fowl, rodents, or insects. Vegans refrain from animal meats as well as from other animal-made foods (such as milk and honey). They also often abstain from buying, wearing or using any kind of animal products (e.g., leather).

Fruit: it represents a vegan diet consisting primarily of fruit.

Raw vegan: This is an uncooked vegan diet that often includes dehydrated foods. Vegetarian: Sometimes, this plant-based diet includes milk and eggs.

Flexitarian: This plant-based diet includes the occasional meat or fish consumption. I like to call it "a little bit of this and a little bit of it" — said, of course, without judgment!

Why You Need To Cut Back On Processed And Animal-Based Products

Youve probably heard that fast food is bad for you over and over again. "Avoid preservatives; avoid processed foods;" but no one really gives you any real or solid information about why they should be avoided and why they are dangerous. So lets break it down so you can fully understand why these guilty culprits should be stopped.

They have huge addictive properties

We have a strong tendency as humans to be addicted to certain foods, but the fact is that it is not our fault entirely. Practically all of the unhealthy foods we indulge in activate our dopamine neurotransmitter brains from time to time. It makes the brain feel "healthy," but this is for only a short time. This also creates a tendency toward addiction; thats why somebody will always find themselves going back to another candy bar-even if they dont really need it. Through cutting the stimulus entirely, you will stop all this.

They are loaded sugar and high fructose corn syrup

Processed and animals based products are loaded with sugars and high fructose corn syrup with a nutritional value that is close to zero. More and more studies are now showing what many people have always suspected; that genetically modified foods cause inflammation of the gut, which in turn makes it more difficult for the body to absorb essential nutrients. The downside of your body, from muscle loss and brain fog to fat gain, cannot be stressed enough if you fail to properly absorb essential nutrients.

They are loaded with refined carbohydrates

Processed foods are loaded with refined carbs and products based on animals. Yes, it is a fact that carbs are needed in your body to provide energy to perform body functions. However, the refining of carbs eliminates the essential nutrients; it eliminates the whole grain component by refining whole grains. After refining, what youre left with is whats called "empty" carbs. By spiking blood sugar and insulin levels, these can have a negative impact on your metabolism.

They are loaded with artificial ingredients

Your body treats them as a foreign object when you consume artificial ingredients. They become an invader in essence. The body is not used to accept things like sucralose or artificial sweeteners. So, your body is doing the best it can. It triggers an immune response that reduces your resistance to disease, making you vulnerable. Otherwise, your bodys focus and energy on protecting your immune system could be diverted elsewhere.

They contain components that cause a hyper reward sense in your body

What this means is that they contain components such as monosodium glutamate (MSG), highfructose corn syrup components, and certain colors that can carve addictive properties. They are encouraging your body to receive a reward from it. For example, MSG is present in many prepackaged pastries. What this does is that to enjoy the taste, it stimulates your taste buds. Just by the way your brain communicates with your taste buds, it becomes psychological.

This reward-based system makes your body want more and more, putting you at a severe risk of over-consumption of calories. What about food from animals? The term "low quality" is often used to refer to plant proteins as they tend to have lower amounts of essential amino acids than animal proteins. What most people dont realize is that more essential amino acids can be harmful to their health. Now, lets discuss more on that.

Animal Protein Lacks Fiber

Most people end up displacing the plant protein they already had in their quest to load more animal protein. This is poor because, unlike plant protein, animal protein lacks fiber, antioxidants, and phytonutrients. Fiber deficiency in various communities and societies around the world is quite common. According to the Institute of Medicine, for instance, in the USA, the average adult absorbs only about 15 grams of fiber per day relative to the 38 grams required. Lack of adequate intake of dietary fiber is associated with increased risk of colon and breast cancer, as well as disease of Crohn, heart disease, and constipation.

Animal protein causes a spike in IGF-1

IGF-1 is the growth factor-1-like hormone insulin. It stimulates cell division and growth, which may sound good but also stimulates cancer cell growth. Therefore, higher blood levels of IGF-1 are associated with increased risk of cancer, malignancy, and proliferation. Animal protein causes phosphorus to increase

Animal protein contains high levels of phosphorus

By secreting a hormone called fibroblast growth factor 23 (FGF23), our bodies normalize the high levels of phosphorus. FGF23 was also found to cause irregular heart muscle enlargement–a risk factor in extreme cases of heart failure and even death.

Instead, given all the issues, the "high quality" of animal proteins aspect might be more appropriately described as "high risk." Like caffeine, which you will feel withdrawal symptoms after you completely cut it off, processed foods can be cut off immediately. Maybe the one thing youre going to lose is the comfort of not having to prepare every meal from scratch.

Plant-Based Diet Vs. Vegan

Mistaking a vegan diet for a plant-based diet is quite common for people or vice versa. Okay, although there are parallels between both diets, they are not quite the same. So lets really break it down quickly.

Vegan

A vegan diet is one that does not include products based on animals. This includes meat, dairy, eggs, and products or ingredients such as honey derived from animals. Someone who describes himself as a vegan carries this perspective into their daily lives. What this means is that they are not using or encouraging the use of clothing, boots, accessories, shampoos, and make-ups made from animal products. For example, wool, beeswax, leather, gelatin, silk, and lanolin are included. Peoples inspiration to live a vegan lifestyle also comes from an urge to stand up and fight animal mistreatment and bad animal ethical treatment, as well as to support animal rights.

Plant-Based Diet

On the other hand, an entire diet based on food plants shares a similarity with veganism in the sense that it does not also promote the dietary consumption of products based on animals. It covers eggs, meat, and dairy. Whats more, unlike the vegan diet, the diet does not include processed foods, white flour, oils, and refined sugars. The aim here is to create a diet of unprocessed vegetables, herbs, whole grains, nuts, seeds and legumes that are minimally processed.

The health benefits it offers are often guided by full-food plant-based diet followers. It is a diet that has very little to do with calorie restriction or macro counting, but mostly with disease prevention and reversal.

Getting Started On A Whole Food Plant-Based Diet

Common misconceptions among many people–even some in the health and fitness industry is that anyone who switches to a plant-based diet becomes super healthy automatically. There are plenty of plant-based junk foods out there, such as non-dairy ice cream and frozen veggie pizza, which can really destroy your health goals if you consume them all the time. The only way you can achieve health benefits is to commit to healthy foods. On the other hand, in keeping you inspired, these plant-based snacks play a role. In moderation, sparingly and in small bits, they should be consumed. Theres a section dedicated to giving suggestions on plant-based snacks that you can cook up at home, as youll see later in this book. So, this is how you get started on a whole plant-based recipe without further ado.

Decide What a Plant-Based Diet Means for You

The first step is to make a decision to structure how your plant-based diet will look, and it will help you transition from your current dietary outlook. This is really personal, something that varies from person to person. While some people choose not to tolerate any animal products at all, some occasionally make do with tiny bits of milk or meat. Deciding what and how you want your plant-based diet to look like is really up to you. The most important thing is that you must make a large majority of your diet from whole plant-based foods.

Understand What You Are Eating

Okay, now that you have taken the decision, your next step will require a great deal of analysis on your side. What do we meaning by this? Well, if this is your first time trying out the plantbased diet, you may be surprised by the number of foods that contain animal products, especially packaged foods. When shopping, youll find yourself cultivating the habit of reading tags. This points out that many pre-packaged foods contain animal products, and if you only want to stick to plant products for your new diet, you need to keep a close eye on the labeling of the ingredients. Maybe youve decided to allow a certain amount of animal products in your diet; well, youre just going to have to watch out for foods filled with oils, sugars, salt, preservatives, and other items that might have an effect on your healthy diet.

Find Revamped Versions of Your Favorite Recipes

Im sure youve got a number of favorite, not necessarily plant-based dishes. Leaving everything behind is typically the hardest part for most people. Theres still a way to meet you halfway, though. Take some time to talk about those non-plant-based foods that you like. Think along the lines of flavor, texture, versatility, and so on; and look for swaps in the entire diet based on food plants that can fulfill what youre missing.

Build a Support Network

Its hard to build a new habit, but it doesnt have to be. Find some friends, or even family members, who are happy to be with you in this lifestyle. This will help you stay focused and inspired while also having a form of transparency and emotional support. You can do fun things like trying out and sharing with these friends new recipes or even hitting up restaurants that offer a variety of plant-based choices. You can even go a step further and look up local social media plant-based groups to help you expand your network of knowledge and support.

Valuable vegetables

Youll find a whole variety of vegetables that youll really get to know quite well when eating plant-based veggies. If youre new to this, at the beginning, youre likely to stick to tried and true, popular veggies because theyre going to feel healthy. These vegetables are a good start:

Beets
Carrots
Kale
Parsley, basil, and other herbs
Spinach
Squash
Sweet potatoes

Fantastic fruits

We all love it! You need to get on this train if you havent because the fruits are delicious; sweet; full of sugar, color, and beautiful vitamins; and so, so good for you.

Apples
Avocado
Bananas
Blueberries
Coconut
Mango
Pears
Pineapple
Raspberries
Strawberries

Wonderful whole grains

Consuming whole grains of good quality is a healthy part of a diet based on vegetables. Dont worry; you can still have your pastas and breads, but the key word here is "whole." You dont want the real thing to be polished or stored. When purchasing these items, make sure that the only ingredient is the grain itself. While it is possible to purchase proper whole grains in packaging from the shelf, make sure that you double-check the label to confirm that it is indeed a whole grain (and just a whole grain).

Brown rice
Brown-rice pasta
Quinoa Rolled oats
Sprouted-grain spelt bread

Lovable legumes

Learning to love beans on a plant-based diet is important because they are a great source of food, protein, and fuel. It may take you and your body a while to get used to them, but they will soon be your friends— especially when you find out how great it is to eat them in soups, salads, burgers, and other creative media. Here are some of the best things to begin with:

Black beans
Chickpeas
Kidney beans
Lentils
Split peas

Notable nuts and seeds

A decent handful of nuts is good. But the thing about eating them on a plant-based diet is to make sure theyre unsalted, unoiled, and raw. You can feel free to eat them in moderation alongside your other wonderful plant-based foods as long as you enjoy them in their natural state. Here are the best to begin with:

Almonds
Cashews
Chia seeds
Flaxseeds
Hempseeds
Pumpkin seeds
Sunflower seeds
Walnuts

Mental resistance is one of the biggest challenges people face when they decide to take up a plant-based diet. In reality, maybe you think its too hard, or its just another diet that wont last or produce the results youre hoping for. Eating a plant-based diet isnt just a fad or something youre doing for weight loss or short-term outcomes. This book is about using plants as your fuel to lead a healthier lifestyle. You need to eat at the end of the day, so why not make your meals and snacks fibrous, delicious, and plant-loaded? I truly believe that with the information contained in this book, together with a keen interest in healthy living, you will discover that consuming a plant-based diet is not difficult and that anybody can
Mental resistance is one of the biggest challenges people face when they decide to take up a plant-based diet. In reality, maybe you think its too hard, or its just another diet that wont last or produce the results youre hoping for. Eating a plant-based diet isnt just a fad or something youre doing for weight loss or short-term outcomes. This book is about using plants as your fuel to lead a healthier lifestyle.

Chapter 2: Breakfast Recipes

Chia Seed Smoothie

Servings: 3
Preparation Time: 5 Minutes
Calories: 477
Protein: 8 Grams
Fat: 29 Grams
Carbs: 57 Grams
Ingredients:
¼ Teaspoon Cinnamon
1 Tablespoon Ginger, Fresh & Grated
Pinch Cardamom
1 Tablespoon Chia Seeds
2 Medjool Dates, Pitted
1 Cup Alfalfa Sprouts
1 Cup Water
1 Banana
½ Cup Coconut Milk, Unsweetened
Directions:
Blend everything together until smooth.

Mango Smoothie

Servings: 3
Preparation Time: 5 Minutes
Calories: 376
Protein: 5 Grams
Fat: 2 Grams
Carbs: 95 Grams

Ingredients:
1 Carrot, Peeled & Chopped
1 Cup Strawberries
1 Cup Water
1 Cup Peaches, Chopped
1 Banana, Frozen & sliced
1 Cup Mango, Chopped
Directions:
Blend everything together until smooth.

Quinoa & Chocolate Bowl

Servings: 2
Preparation Time: 35 Minutes
Calories: 392
Protein: 12 Grams
Fat: 19 Grams
Carbs: 49 Grams
Ingredients:
1 Cup Quinoa
1 Cup Almond Milk, Unsweetened
1 Teaspoon Cinnamon
1 Banana
1 Cup Water
2-3 Tablespoons Cocoa Powder, Unsweetened
2 Tablespoons Almond Butter
1 Tablespoon Chia Seeds, Ground
2 Tablespoons Walnuts, Optional
¼ Cup Raspberries, Fresh
Directions:
Place your cinnamon, milk, water and quinoa in a pot, bringing it to a boil before turning it down to low heat to simmer. Cover, simmering for twenty-five to thirty minutes.

Puree your banana, mixing in your almond butter, flaxseed and cocoa powder.

Scoop a cup of quinoa into a bowl, and then top with pudding, raspberries and walnuts if youre using them before serving.

Vegetable Hash

Servings: 4
Preparation Time: 35 Minutes
Calories: 273
Protein: 9 Grams
Fat: 11 Grams
Carbs: 39 Grams
Ingredients:
1 Tablespoon Sage Leaves, Chopped
1 Bell Pepper, Diced
3 Cloves Garlic, Minced
1 Onion, Diced
3 Tablespoons Olive Oil
3 Red Potatoes, Diced
15 Ounces Black Beans, Canned
1 Tablespoon Parsley, Chopped
2 Cups Swiss Chard, Chopped
Sea Salt & Black Pepper to Taste
Directions:
Start by cooking your potato, garlic and onion in a skillet with your oil. This will take twenty minutes.

Add in your Swiss chard and beans, cooking for three more minutes.

Season with salt and pepper, and serve with parsley.

Walnut Porridge

Servings: 2
Preparation Time: 25 Minutes
Calories: 312
Protein: 7 Grams
Fat: 18 Grams
Carbs: 35 Grams
Ingredients:
1 ½ Cups Water
½ Cup Coconut Milk, Unsweetened
1 Cup Teff, Whole Grain
½ Teaspoon Cardamom, Ground
1 Teaspoon Sea Salt, Fine
¼ Cup Walnuts, Chopped
1 Tablespoon Maple Syrup, Pure
Directions:
Start by combining your coconut oil and water, bringing it to a boil before stirring in your teff.
Add the cardamom, and then allow it to simmer for twenty minutes.
Mix in your walnuts and maple syrup before serving.

Granola

Servings: 7
Preparation Time: 1 Hour 30 Minutes
Calories: 239
Protein: 6 Grams
Fat: 11 Grams
Carbs: 32 Grams
Ingredients:
½ Cup Maple Syrup, Pure
¼ Cup Coconut Oil

¾ Cup Coconut, Unsweetened & Shredded
1 Cup Almonds, Slivered
¾ Teaspoon Sea Salt, Fine
5 Cups Rolled Oats
Directions:
Start by heating your oven to 250, and then mix all of your ingredients together in a bowl.
Spread your granola out over two baking sheets, making sure its spread out evenly.
Bake for an hour and fifteen minutes, but youll need to stir every twenty minutes.
Allow it to cool before serving.

Breakfast Cereal

Servings: 6
Preparation Time: 45 Minutes
Calories: 160
Protein: 3 Grams
Fat: 1.5 Grams
Carbs: 34 Grams
Ingredients:
¼ Tablespoon Butter
2 ¼ Cups Water
Honey to Taste
1 Teaspoon Cinnamon
1 Cup Brown Rice, Uncooked
½ Cup Raisins, Seedless
Directions:
Start by combining your cinnamon, raisins, rice, and butter in a saucepan before adding in your water. Bring it to a boil, and allow it to simmer while covered for forty minutes. Fluff with a fork.
Serve with honey.

Fruity Oatmeal

Servings: 2
Preparation Time: 25 Minutes
Calories: 230
Protein: 4.6 Grams
Fat: 5.6 Grams
Carbs: 43.8 Grams
Ingredients:
½ Cup Apple Juice, Fresh & Frozen
½ Cup Oatmeal
½ Cup Water
3 Prunes, Diced
1 Apple, Small & Diced
4 Pecans, Diced
3 Apricots, Dehydrated, Dried & Diced
¼ Teaspoon Cinnamon
Directions:
Start by getting out a small saucepan and mix together your apple juice and water, bringing the mixture to a boil.
Add a half a cup of oatmeal, cooking for a minute. Add in your pecans, cinnamon and fruit pieces. Make sure to stir. If you want to make sure you have more vitamins, add in your fruit when your oatmeal is nearly cool.

Pecan Pumpkin Spice Oatmeal

Preparation Time: 15 Minutes
Servings: 2
Ingredients:
1/2 cup steel-cut oats
1/2 cup pumpkin purée
1 1/2 cups unsweetened almond milk
1/2 teaspoon cinnamon

1/8 teaspoon nutmeg
1 teaspoon vanilla extract
1/8 teaspoon of ground cloves
1/8 teaspoon ginger
1/4 cup brown sugar
Chopped pecans, for serving
Directions:
Spray the instant pot with nonstick spray. Combine everything except for the brown sugar and pecans.
Seal the lid and cook on high 3 minutes, then let the pressure release naturally.
Stir in the brown sugar and top with chopped pecans.

Carrot Cake Oatmeal with Cream Cheese Frosting

Preparation Time: 20 Minutes
Servings: 2
Ingredients:
1 small white sweet potato, peeled and steamed
1 small carrot, grated
1/4 small zucchini, grated
1/2 cup steel-cut oats
1 1/2 cups nondairy milk
1/2 teaspoon lemon juice
1/2 teaspoon apple cider vinegar
1/8 teaspoon of salt
1/8 teaspoon ground cloves
1/8 teaspoon nutmeg
1/2 teaspoon cinnamon
2 tablespoons brown sugar
2 tablespoons maple syrup
1 1/2 tablespoons coconut oil

1 tablespoon water
Directions:
To make the cream cheese frosting, puree half of the steamed sweet potato in a food processor. Add the maple syrup, water, coconut oil, lemon juice, and apple cider vinegar and puree until smooth. Add more sweet potato if the mixture is not thick enough.

Spray the instant pot with nonstick spray. Combine the rest of the ingredients, then seal the lid and cook on high 3 minutes. Let the pressure release naturally. Add additional milk to the oatmeal if needed, and top each serving with a dollop of the cream cheese frosting.

Chocolate Walnut Oatmeal

Preparation Time: 15 Minutes
Servings: 2
Ingredients:
1/2 cup steel-cut oats
2 tablespoons cocoa powder
1 teaspoon brown sugar
1 tablespoon agave nectar
1 teaspoon vanilla extract
1/2 cup unsweetened almond milk
1 1/2 cups water
Semi-sweet chocolate chips, for topping
Walnuts for topping
Directions:
Spray the instant pot with nonstick spray. Combine the oats, cocoa powder, water, vanilla, brown sugar, and agave nectar. Cook on high 3 minutes, then let the pressure release naturally. Stir in the almond milk.
Top with chocolate chips and walnuts.

Breakfast Burrito Filling

Preparation Time: 15 Minutes
Servings: 4
Ingredients:
15 ounces tofu, drained and crumbled
1/2 cup water
1 clove garlic, minced
1/2 bell pepper, chopped
1/2 teaspoon chili powder
1/4 teaspoon chipotle chili powder
1/4 teaspoon sriracha sauce
1 teaspoon lime juice
Salt and pepper, to taste
1/4 cup shredded vegan cheddar cheese, for serving
Warm tortillas, for serving
Salsa, for serving
Directions:
Combine all the ingredients in the instant pot. Seal the lid and cook on high 4 minutes, then let the pressure release naturally.
If the mixture is too wet, drain off some of the water. Stir in the cheese to melt it. Serve wrapped warm tortillas with salsa.

Tofu Breakfast Custard and Potatoes

Preparation Time: 25 Minutes
Servings: 4
Ingredients:
12 ounces frozen hash browns
1 shallot, chopped
2 tablespoons vegan chicken-flavored bouillon
10 ounces silken tofu

1/2 cup shredded vegan cheddar cheese
1/2 cup nondairy milk
1/4 teaspoon onion powder
1/8 teaspoon garlic powder
1/2 teaspoon seasoned salt
1/4 teaspoon freshly ground pepper
1 tablespoon olive oil
Hot sauce, for serving
Directions:
Puree the tofu, milk, bouillon, garlic powder, onion powder and seasoned salt in a food processor.
Heat the oil in the instant pot on the sauté setting and cook the shallot for 3 minutes.
Spread the hash browns on top of the cooked shallots, and top with the cheese. Pour the tofu puree over the top, then sprinkle with fresh ground pepper.
Cook on high 5 minutes, then quick release the pressure.
The tofu mixture should be a jiggly custard texture. If it is too moist, return the instant pot to the sauté setting and cook longer with the lid on but vented.
Serve with hot sauce!

Apple and Sausage French Toast Casserole

Preparation Time: 25 Minutes
Servings: 4
Ingredients:
4 links vegan breakfast sausages, chopped into coins
2 apples, peeled and chopped
Juice of 1/2 lemon
Zest of 1/2 lemon
1/2 loaf whole wheat bread, chopped into cubes
1 1/2 cups water
1 teaspoon vanilla extract

3 tablespoons unsweetened applesauce
1/2 teaspoon cinnamon
1 tablespoon olive oil
Maple syrup, for serving

Directions:

Heat olive oil in the instant pot using the sauté setting. Add the sausage and cook for 10 minutes.

Add the water, applesauce, vanilla extract, lemon juice, and cinnamon to the instant pot. Add the apples, then the bread cubes. Push the bread down to make sure it is all coated with the mixture.

Seal the lid and cook on high 4 minutes, then let the pressure release naturally. Dust with powdered sugar and lemon zest and serve.

Granola

Preparation Time: 25 Minutes
Servings: 8 cups

Ingredients:

5 cups old-fashioned rolled oats
1 cup slivered blanched almonds
⅔ cup pure maple syrup
½ cup wheat germ
½ cup unsweetened shredded coconut
½ cup sunflower seeds
½ cup golden raisins or sweetened dried cranberries
½ cup chopped dates or dried apricots
¼ cup vegetable oil
¼ cup packed light brown sugar
3 tablespoons water
1 teaspoon pure vanilla extract

Directions:

Spray the Instant Pot insert with cooking spray and set to high.
Add the maple syrup, oil, water, sugar, and vanilla.
In a bowl combine the oats, wheat germ, almonds, sunflower seeds, coconut, and dates.
Mix the oats into the syrup mix in the Instant Pot.
Seal and cook on Meat for 12 minutes.
Release the pressure and cook with the lid open until your granola is crisp.

Granola Oats

Preparation Time: 50 Minutes
Servings: 4
Ingredients:
4½ cups water
1¼ cups old-fashioned rolled oats or steel-cut oats
1 cup granola
1½ teaspoons ground cinnamon
½ teaspoon salt
Directions:
Lightly oil your Instant Pot insert with cooking spray.
Combine the oats, water, cinnamon, and salt.
Seal and cook on Stew for 40 minutes.
Release the pressure naturally and stir in the granola.
36. Spiced Apple Oats.
Preparation Time: 50 Minutes
Servings: 4
Ingredients:
3 cups water
2 cups apple juice
2 apples, peeled, cored, and chopped
1¼ cups steel-cut oats
½ cup golden raisins or dried cranberries

¼ cup packed light brown sugar or granulated natural sugar, or more to taste
1 tablespoon ground flaxseed
1 teaspoon ground cinnamon
½ teaspoon salt
Directions:
Lightly oil your Instant Pot insert with cooking spray.
Combine the ingredients.
Seal and cook on Stew for 40 minutes.

PB&J Oats

Preparation Time: 50 Minutes
Servings: 6
Ingredients:
5½ cups water
1½ cups steel-cut oats
½ cup strawberry jam
½ cup creamy peanut butter, at room temperature
1 teaspoon ground cinnamon
¾ teaspoon salt
Directions:
Lightly oil your Instant Pot insert with cooking spray.
Combine the oats, water, cinnamon, and salt.
Seal and cook on Stew for 40 minutes.
Release the pressure naturally and stir in the peanut butter and jam.

Choco-Coco Milk Shake

Preparation Time: 25 MIN

Servings: 1
Ingredients:
½ cup whole milk
1 tbsp cocoa powder
1 packet Stevia, or more to taste
1 tbsp coconut flakes, unsweetened
1 cup water
1 tbsp coconut oil
Directions:
Add all ingredients in blender.
Blend until smooth and creamy.
Serve and enjoy.
Nutrition:
Calories per serving: 263; Carbohydrates: 22.7g; Protein: 4.8g; Fat: 20.65g; Sugar: 14.7g; Sodium: 75mg; Fiber: 2.1g

Nutty Choco Milk Shake

Preparation Time: 25 MIN
Servings: 1
Ingredients:
¼ cup whole milk
1 tbsp cocoa powder
1 packet Stevia, or more to taste
¼ cup pecans
1 ½ cups water
1 tbsp macadamia oil
Directions:
Add all ingredients in blender.
Blend until smooth and creamy.
Serve and enjoy.
Nutrition:
Calories per serving: 358; Carbohydrates: 15.5g; Protein: 5.1g; Fat: 34.0g; Sugar: 8.9g; Sodium: 33mg; Fiber: 4g

Gritty Choco Milk Shake

Preparation Time: 25 MIN
Servings: 1
Ingredients:
¼ cup whole milk
1 tbsp cocoa powder
1 packet Stevia, or more to taste
1 tbsp chia seeds
1 tbsp hemp seeds
1 tbsp flaxseed
1 ½ cups water
1 tbsp Flaxseed oil
Directions:
Add all ingredients in blender.
Blend until creamy yet still gritty. If preferred, blend until smooth.
Serve and enjoy.
Nutrition:
Calories per serving: 363; Carbohydrates: 22.8g; Protein: 8.9g; Fat: 29.4g; Sugar: 8.3g; Sodium: 42mg; Fiber: 10.1g

Creamy Choco Shake

Preparation Time: 25 MIN
Servings: 1
Ingredients:
½ cup heavy cream
2 tbsps cocoa powder
1 packet Stevia, or more to taste

1 cup water
Directions:
Add all ingredients in blender.
Blend until smooth and creamy.
Serve and enjoy.
Nutrition:
Calories per serving: 435; Carbohydrates: 10.6g; Protein: 4.6g; Fat: 45.5g; Sugar: 3.5g; Sodium: 52mg; Fiber: 4g

Raspberry-Choco Shake

Preparation Time: 25 MINUTES
Servings: 1
Ingredients:
½ cup heavy cream, liquid
1 tbsp cocoa powder
1 packet Stevia, or more to taste
¼ cup raspberries
1 ½ cups water
Directions:
Add all ingredients in blender.
Blend until smooth and creamy.
Serve and enjoy.
Nutrition:
Calories per serving: 438; Carbohydrates: 11.1g; Protein: 3.8g; Fat: 45.0g; Sugar: 4.8g; Sodium: 54mg; Fiber: 3.6g

Strawberry-Choco Shake

Preparation Time: 25 MINUTES
Servings: 1

Ingredients:
½ cup heavy cream, liquid
1 tbsp cocoa powder
1 packet Stevia, or more to taste
½ cup strawberry, sliced
1 tbsp coconut flakes, unsweetened
1 ½ cups water
Directions:
Add all ingredients in blender.
Blend until smooth and creamy.
Serve and enjoy.
Nutrition:
Calories per serving: 470; Carbohydrates: 15.7g; Protein: 4.1g; Fat: 46.4g; Sugar: 8.9g; Sodium: 69mg; Fiber: 3.6g

Almond Choco Shake

Preparation Time: 25 MINUTES
Servings: 1
Ingredients:
½ cup heavy cream, liquid
1 tbsp cocoa powder
1 packet Stevia, or more to taste
½ cup almonds, chopped
1 ½ cups water
Directions:
Soak almonds in water for at least 30 minutes.
Then, add all ingredients in blender.
Blend until smooth and creamy.
Serve and enjoy.
Nutrition:
Calories per serving: 485; Carbohydrates: 15.7g; Protein: 11.9g; Fat: 45.9g; Sugar: 3.8g; Sodium: 31mg; Fiber: 7.4g

Gritty and Nutty Shake

Preparation Time: 25 MINUTES
Servings: 1
Ingredients:
¼ cup heavy cream, liquid
½ tbsp cocoa powder
1 packet Stevia, or more to taste
¼ cup almonds, sliced
¼ cup macadamia nuts, whole
1 tbsp flaxseed
1 tbsp hemp seed
1 cup water
Directions:
Add all ingredients in blender.
Blend until smooth and creamy.
Serve and enjoy.
Nutrition:
Calories per serving: 590; Carbohydrates: 17.7g; Protein: 12.3g; Fat: 57.2g; Sugar: 3.8g; Sodium: 22mg; Fiber: 10.1g

Nutty Greens Shake
Servings: 1
Ingredients:
½ cup heavy cream, liquid
1 packet Stevia, or more to taste
¼ cup pecans
¼ macadamia nuts
1 ½ cups water
1 cup Spring mix salad greens
Directions:
Add all ingredients in blender.
Blend until smooth and creamy.
Serve and enjoy.

Nutrition:
Calories per serving: 628; Carbohydrates: 12.5g; Protein: 7.0g; Fat: 65.6g; Sugar: 4.7g; Sodium: 48mg; Fiber: 6.4g

Raspberry and Greens Shake

Preparation Time: 20 MINUTES
Servings: 1
Ingredients:
1 cup whole milk
1 packet Stevia, or more to taste
¼ cup Raspberry
1 cup water
1 tbsp macadamia oil
1 cup Spinach
Directions:
Add all ingredients in blender.
Blend until smooth and creamy.
Serve and enjoy.
Nutrition:
Calories per serving: 292; Carbohydrates: 17.43g; Protein: 8.9g; Fat: 21.9g; Sugar: 13.8g; Sodium: 136mg; Fiber: 2.7g

Spiced Almond Shake

Preparation Time: 20 MINUTES
Servings: 1
Ingredients:
½ cup whole milk
1 tbsp cocoa powder
1 packet Stevia, or more to taste
¼ cup almonds, sliced
½ tsp cinnamon

¼ tsp allspice
¼ tsp nutmeg
1 cup water
1 tbsp almond oil
Directions:
Add all ingredients in blender.
Blend until smooth and creamy.
Serve and enjoy.
Nutrition:
Calories per serving: 347; Carbohydrates: 16.6g; Protein: 9.8g; Fat: 30.1g; Sugar: 7.3g; Sodium: 59mg; Fiber: 5.4g

Cinnamon-Choco Coffee Milk Shake

Preparation Time: 20 Minutes
Servings: 1
Ingredients:
1 cup whole milk
1 tbsp cocoa powder
1 cup brewed coffee, chilled
½ tsp cinnamon
1 packet Stevia, or more to taste
1 tbsp coconut oil
Directions:
Add all ingredients in blender.
Blend until smooth and creamy.
Serve and enjoy.
Nutrition:
Calories per serving: 284; Carbohydrates: 16.9g; Protein: 9g; Fat: 22.3g; Sugar: 12.4g; Sodium: 111mg; Fiber: 2.3g

Mocha Milk Shake

Preparation Time: 20 Minutes
Servings: 1
Ingredients:
1 cup whole milk
2 tbsps cocoa powder
2 packet Stevia, or more to taste
1 cup brewed coffee, chilled
1 tbsp coconut oil
Directions:
Add all ingredients in blender.
Blend until smooth and creamy.
Serve and enjoy.
Nutrition:
Calories per serving: 293; Carbohydrates: 19.9g; Protein: 10.1g; Fat: 23.1g; Sugar: 12.5g; Sodium: 112mg; Fiber: 4g

Coconut-Mocha Shake

Preparation Time: 20 Minutes
Servings: 1
Ingredients:
3/4 cup whole milk
2 tbsps cocoa powder
1 tbsp coconut flakes, unsweetened
2 packet Stevia, or more to taste
1 cup brewed coffee, chilled
1 tbsp coconut oil
Directions:
Add all ingredients in blender.
Blend until smooth and creamy.
Serve and enjoy.
Nutrition:

Calories per serving: 280; Carbohydrates: 19.75g; Protein: 8.33g; Fat: 22.6g; Sugar: 11.4g; Sodium: 101mg; Fiber: 4.5g

Nutritiously Green Milk Shake

Preparation Time: 20 Minutes
Servings: 1
Ingredients:
1 cup whole milk
1 packet Stevia, or more to taste
1 tbsp coconut flakes, unsweetened
1 cup water
2 cups Spring Mix Salad
1 tbsp coconut oil
Directions:
Add all ingredients in blender.
Blend until smooth and creamy.
Serve and enjoy.
Nutrition:
Calories per serving: 309; Carbohydrates: 18.9g; Protein: 9.5g; Fat: 23.3g; Sugar: 15.3g; Sodium: 157mg; Fiber: 2.7g

Strawberry-Spinach Shake

Preparation Time: 20 Minutes
Servings: 1
Ingredients:
½ cup whole milk yogurt
1 cup spinach
1 packet Stevia, or more to taste
1 tbsp MCT oil

½ cup strawberries, chopped
1 tbsp hemp seeds
1 tbsp flaxseed, ground
1 ½ cups water
Directions:
Add all ingredients in blender.
Blend until smooth and creamy.
Serve and enjoy.
Nutrition:
Calories per serving: 334; Carbohydrates: 18.9g; Protein: 9.4g; Fat: 26.7g; Sugar: 10.3g; Sodium: 90mg; Fiber: 5.9g

Lemon-Mint Creamy Green Smoothie

Preparation Time: 20 Minutes
Servings: 1
Ingredients:
½ cup whole milk yogurt
1 cup Spring mix salad greens, packed
1 packet Stevia, or more to taste
1 tbsp MCT oil
1 tsp lemon juice, fresh
2 peppermint leaves
1 tbsp chia seeds
1 tbsp flaxseed, ground
1 ½ cups water
Directions:
Add all ingredients in blender.
Blend until smooth and creamy.
Serve and enjoy.
Nutrition:
Calories per serving: 326; Carbohydrates: 17.1g; Protein: 9.4g; Fat: 26.3g; Sugar: 6.1g; Sodium: 91mg; Fiber: 8.4g

5-Lettuce Mix Green Shake

Preparation Time: 20 Minutes
Servings: 1
Ingredients:
¾ cup whole milk yogurt
2 cups 5-lettuce mix salad greens
1 packet Stevia, or more to taste
1 tbsp MCT oil
1 tbsp chia seeds
1 ½ cups water
Directions:
Add all ingredients in blender.
Blend until smooth and creamy.
Serve and enjoy.
Nutrition:
Calories per serving: 320; Carbohydrates: 19.1g; Protein: 10.4g; Fat: 24.2g; Sugar: 9.6g; Sodium: 126mg; Fiber: 7.1g

Basil and Pine Nuts Shake

Preparation Time: 20 Minutes
Servings: 1
Ingredients:
½ cup whole milk yogurt
1 cup spring mix salad greens
1 packet Stevia, or more to taste
1 tbsp olive oil
2 tbsps pine nuts, chopped
2 tbsps walnuts, chopped

10 basil leaves
1 tbsp hemp seeds
1 ½ cups water
Directions:
Add all ingredients in blender.
Blend until smooth and creamy.
Serve and enjoy.
Nutrition:
Calories per serving: 465; Carbohydrates: 14.6g; Protein: 11.6g; Fat: 43.2g; Sugar: 7.4g; Sodium: 81mg; Fiber: 3.5g

Rosemary-Lemon Garden Greens Smoothie

Preparation Time: 20 Minutes
Servings: 1
Ingredients:
½ cup whole milk yogurt
1 cup Garden greens
1 packet Stevia, or more to taste
1 tbsp olive oil
1 stalk fresh rosemary
1 tbsp lemon juice, fresh
1 tbsp pepitas
1 tbsp flaxseed, ground
1 ½ cups water
Directions:
Add all ingredients in blender.
Blend until smooth and creamy.
Serve and enjoy.
Nutrition:
Calories per serving: 312; Carbohydrates: 14.7g; Protein: 9.7g; Fat: 25.9g; Sugar: 8.6g; Sodium: 75mg; Fiber: 4g

Lemon-Cilantro Greens Shake

Preparation Time: 20 Minutes
Servings: 1
Ingredients:
½ cup whole milk yogurt
1 cup baby kale greens
1 packet Stevia, or more to taste
1 tbsp avocado oil
1 tbsp lemon juice, fresh
1 tsp cilantro, chopped
¼ avocado fruit
1 tbsp flaxseed, ground
1 ½ cups water
Directions:
Add all ingredients in blender.
Blend until smooth and creamy.
Serve and enjoy.
Nutrition:
Calories per serving: 345; Carbohydrates: 16.4g; Protein: 7.9g; Fat: 29.9g; Sugar: 6.9g; Sodium: 76mg; Fiber: 6.8g

Blackberry-Chocolate Shake

Preparation Time: 20 Minutes
Servings: 1
Ingredients:
½ cup whole milk yogurt
¼ cup blackberries
1 packet Stevia, or more to taste
1 tbsp MCT oil
1 tbsp Dutch-processed cocoa powder
2 tbsps Macadamia nuts, chopped
1 ½ cups water

Directions:
Add all ingredients in blender.
Blend until smooth and creamy.
Serve and enjoy.
Nutrition:
Calories per serving: 463; Carbohydrates: 17.9g; Protein: 8.5g; Fat: 43.9g; Sugar: 9.1g; Sodium: 67mg; Fiber: 6.8g

Strawberry-Coconut Shake

Preparation Time: 20 Min
Servings: 1
Ingredients:
½ cup whole milk yogurt
1 packet Stevia, or more to taste
1 tbsp MCT oil
¼ cup strawberries, chopped
1 tbsp coconut flakes, unsweetened
1 tbsp hemp seeds
1 ½ cups water
Directions:
Add all ingredients in blender.
Blend until smooth and creamy.
Serve and enjoy.
Nutrition:
Calories per serving: 282; Carbohydrates: 14.0g; Protein: 6.5g; Fat: 23.7g; Sugar: 9.6g; Sodium: 80mg; Fiber: 2g

Coconut-Melon Yogurt Shake

Preparation Time: 20 Min
Servings: 1
Ingredients:

¼ cup whole milk yogurt
1 packet Stevia, or more to taste
1 tbsp coconut oil
½ cup melon, slices
1 tbsp coconut flakes, unsweetened
1 tbsp chia seeds
1 ½ cups water
Directions:
Add all ingredients in blender.
Blend until smooth and creamy.
Serve and enjoy.
Nutrition:
Calories per serving: 278; Carbohydrates: 19.8g; Protein: 5.4g; Fat: 21.6g; Sugar: 11.8g; Sodium: 67mg; Fiber: 6.2g

Berry Nutty Shake

Preparation Time: 20 Min
Servings: 1
Ingredients:
½ cup whole milk yogurt
1 packet Stevia, or more to taste
¼ cup boysenberries
¼ cup Blackberry
¼ cup strawberries, chopped
1 tbsp hemp seeds
1 tbsp pepitas
1 tbsp chia seeds
1 ½ cups water
Directions:
Add all ingredients in blender.
Blend until smooth and creamy.
Serve and enjoy.
Nutrition:

Calories per serving: 283; Carbohydrates: 26.2g; Protein: 11.8g; Fat: 16.9g; Sugar: 12.1g; Sodium: 69mg; Fiber: 10.6g

Berry Overload Shake

Preparation Time: 20 Min
Servings: 1
Ingredients:
½ cup whole milk yogurt
1 packet Stevia, or more to taste
¼ cup blueberries
¼ cup boysenberries
¼ cup Blackberry
¼ cup strawberries, chopped
1 tbsp avocado oil
1 ½ cups water
Directions:
Add all ingredients in blender.
Blend until smooth and creamy.
Serve and enjoy.
Nutrition:
Calories per serving: 263; Carbohydrates: 22.3g; Protein: 5.6g; Fat: 18.5g; Sugar: 15.2g; Sodium: 65mg; Fiber: 5.3g

Berry-Choco Goodness Shake

Preparation Time: 20 Min
Servings: 1
Ingredients:
½ cup whole milk yogurt
1 packet Stevia, or more to taste

¼ cup raspberries
¼ cup Blackberry
¼ cup strawberries, chopped
1 tbsp cocoa powder
1 tbsp avocado oil
1 ½ cups water
Directions:
Add all ingredients in blender.
Blend until smooth and creamy.
Serve and enjoy.
Nutrition:
Calories per serving: 255; Carbohydrates: 20.2g; Protein: 6.4g; Fat: 19.2g; Sugar: 11.0g; Sodium: 66mg; Fiber: 6.3g

Lemony-Avocado Cilantro Shake

Preparation Time: 20 Min
Servings: 1
Ingredients:
½ cup whole milk yogurt
1 packet Stevia, or more to taste
1 whole avocado
1 tbsp chopped cilantro
1 ½ cups water
Directions:
Add all ingredients in blender.
Blend until smooth and creamy.
Serve and enjoy.
Nutrition:
Calories per serving: 397; Carbohydrates: 23.4g; Protein: 8.3g; Fat: 33.4g; Sugar: 7.0g; Sodium: 78mg; Fiber: 13.5g

Strawberry-Chocolate Yogurt Shake

Preparation Time: 20 Min
Servings: 1
Ingredients:
½ cup whole milk yogurt
1 packet Stevia, or more to taste
½ cup strawberries, chopped
1 tbsp cocoa powder
1 tbsp coconut oil
1 tbsp pepitas
1 ½ cups water
Directions:
Add all ingredients in blender.
Blend until smooth and creamy.
Serve and enjoy.
Nutrition:
Calories per serving: 269; Carbohydrates: 16.5g; Protein: g; Fat: 7.9g; Sugar: 9.4g; Sodium: 67mg; Fiber: 3.5g

Blueberry and Greens Smoothie

Preparation Time: 20 Min
Servings: 1
Ingredients:
½ cup coconut milk
1 ½ cups water
½ cup blueberries
2 packets Stevia, or as needed
1 cup arugula
1 tbsp hemp seeds
Directions:
Add all ingredients in blender.
Blend until smooth and creamy.

Serve and enjoy.
Nutrition:
Calories per serving: 321; Carbohydrates: 18.4g; Protein: 5.2g; Fat: 29.0g; Sugar: 8.0g; Sodium: 29mg; Fiber: 2.9g

Avocado and Greens Smoothie

Preparation Time: 20 Min
Servings: 1
Ingredients:
½ cup coconut milk
1 ½ cups water
½ Avocado fruit
2 packets Stevia, or as needed
1 cup Spring mix greens
1 tbsp avocado oil
Directions:
Add all ingredients in blender.
Blend until smooth and creamy.
Serve and enjoy.
Nutrition:
Calories per serving: 439; Carbohydrates: 16.1g; Protein: 6.5g; Fat: 43.4g; Sugar: 1.0g; Sodium: 37mg; Fiber: 7.7g

Chapter 3. Soup Recipes

Cauliflower Soup

Preparation Time: 10 minutes
Cooking Time: 4 hours 5 minutes
Servings: 04
Ingredients:
2 tablespoons olive oil
1½ cups sweet white onion, chopped
2 large cloves of garlic, chopped
1 head cauliflower, cut into florets
1 cup coconut milk
1 cup filtered water
1 teaspoon vegetable stock paste
2 tablespoons nutritional yeast
Dash of olive oil
Fresh cracked pepper
Parsley, to serve
Directions:
Add olive oil and onion to a slow cooker.
Sauté for 5 minutes then add the rest of the ingredients.
Put on the slow cookers lid and cook for 4 hours on low heat.
Once done, blend the soup with a hand blender.
Garnish with parsley, and cracked pepper
Serve.
Nutrition:
Calories 119
Total Fat 14 g
Saturated Fat 2 g
Cholesterol 65 mg
Sodium 269 mg

Total Carbs 19 g
Fiber 4 g
Sugar 6 g
Protein 5g

Greek Lentil Soup

Preparation Time: 10 minutes
Cooking Time: 6 hours 2 minutes
Servings: 04
Ingredients:
Soup:
1 cup lentils
1 medium sweet onion, chopped
2 large carrots, chopped
2 sticks of celery, chopped
4 cups veggie broth
Olive oil to sauté
4 tablespoons tomato sauce
3 cloves garlic
3 bay leaves
Salt, to taste
Black pepper, to taste
Dried oregano, to taste
Toppings:
Vinegar
Lemon juice
Hot sauce
Directions:
In a slow cooker, add olive oil and onion.
Sauté for 2 minutes then add the rest of the soup ingredients.
Put on the slow cookers lid and cook for 6 hours on low heat.

Serve warm with the vinegar, lemon juice, and hot sauce.
Nutrition:
Calories 231
Total Fat 20.1 g
Saturated Fat 2.4 g
Cholesterol 110 mg
Sodium 941 mg
Total Carbs 20.1 g
Fiber 0.9 g
Sugar 1.4 g
Protein 4.6 g

Broccoli White Bean Soup

Preparation Time: 10 minutes
Cooking Time: 4 hrs. 32 minutes
Servings: 04
Ingredients:
1 large bunch broccoli
3 cloves garlic
1 medium white potato
¼ cup carrot, chopped
2 cups almond milk
1½ cups white beans, cooked
1 white onion, chopped
¾ teaspoon black pepper
¼ teaspoon salt
½ teaspoon smoky paprika
⅓ cup nutritional yeast
1 bay leaf
1 cup cooked pasta
Directions:

In a slow cooker, add olive oil and onion.
Sauté for 2 minutes then toss in the rest of the ingredients except pasta and beans.
Put on the slow cookers lid and cook for 4 hours on low heat.
Once done, add pasta and beans to the soup and mix gently.
Cover the soup and remove it from the heat then leave it for another 30 minutes.
Serve warm.
Nutrition:
Calories 361
Total Fat 16.3 g
Saturated Fat 4.9 g
Cholesterol 114 mg
Sodium 515 mg
Total Carbs 29.3 g
Fiber 0.1 g
Sugar 18.2 g
Protein 3.3 g

African Lentil Soup

Preparation Time: 10 minutes
Cooking Time: 20 minutes
Servings: 4
Ingredients:
1 teaspoon oil
½ medium onion, chopped
2 juicy tomatoes, chopped
1½ teaspoons ground cumin
4 garlic cloves, chopped
1-inch piece of ginger, chopped
1 tablespoon Sambal Oelek
¼ teaspoon black pepper

1 teaspoon Harissa Spice Blend
¼ cup nut butter
2 tablespoons peanuts
½ cup red lentils
2 teaspoons ground coriander
2½ cups vegetable stock
1 tablespoon tomato paste
¾ teaspoon salt
1 teaspoon lemon juice
½ cup packed baby spinach
Directions:
In a slow cooker, add olive oil and onion.
Sauté for 5 minutes then toss in rest of the ingredients except peanuts.
Put on the slow cookers lid and cook for 5 hours on low heat.
Once done, garnish with peanuts.
Serve.
Nutrition:
Calories 205
Total Fat 22.7 g
Saturated Fat 6.1 g
Cholesterol 4 mg
Sodium 227 mg
Total Carbs 26.1 g
Fiber 1.4 g
Sugar 0.9 g
Protein 5.2 g

Artichoke Bean Soup

Preparation Time: 10 minutes
Cooking Time: 20 minutes
Servings: 04

Ingredients:
1 (15 ounce) can artichoke hearts
½ bunch kale, chopped
2 cups vegetable broth
1 tablespoon dried basil
1 tablespoon dried oregano
1 teaspoon salt
½ teaspoon red pepper flakes
Black pepper, to taste
2 (14 ounce) cans roasted tomatoes, diced
1 (15 ounce) can white beans, drained

Directions:
Add all ingredients to a saucepan.
Put on the saucepans lid and cook for 20 minutes on a simmer.
Serve warm.

Nutrition:
Calories 201
Total Fat 8.9 g
Saturated Fat 4.5 g
Cholesterol 57 mg
Sodium 340 mg
Total Carbs 24.7 g
Fiber 1.2 g
Sugar 1.3 g
Protein 15.3 g

Chinese Rice Soup

Preparation Time: 10 minutes
Cooking Time: 3 hrs.
Servings: 04
Ingredients:

Congee:
1 cup of white rice (uncooked)
2-inch piece fresh ginger, minced
4 cloves garlic, minced
10 cups water
14 dried shiitake mushrooms
Toppings:
Green onions
Cilantro
Sesame seeds
Hot sauce
Toasted sesame oil
Soy sauce
Peanuts
Chili oil
Shelled edamame
Directions:
Add all the ingredients to a slow cooker.
Put on the slow cookers lid and cook for 3 hours on low heat.
Once done, garnish with desired toppings.
Serve warm.
Nutrition:
Calories 210.6
Total Fat 10.91g
Saturated Fat 7.4g
Sodium 875 mg
Potassium 604 mg
Carbohydrates 25.6g
Fiber 4.3g
Sugar 7.9g
Protein 2.1g

Black-eyed Pea Soup with Greens

Preparation Time: 10 minutes
Cooking Time: 5 hrs.
Servings: 04
Ingredients:
½ cup black eyed peas
½ cup brown lentils
1 teaspoon oil
½ teaspoon cumin seeds
½ cup onions, chopped
5 cloves garlic, chopped
1-inch piece of ginger chopped
1 teaspoon ground coriander
½ teaspoon ground cumin
½ teaspoon turmeric
¼ teaspoon black pepper
½ teaspoon cayenne powder
2 tomatoes, chopped
½ teaspoon lemon juice
1 teaspoon salt
2 ½ cups water
½ cup chopped spinach
½ cup small chopped green beans
Directions:
Add olive oil and cumin seeds to a slow cooker.
Sauté for 1 minute then toss in the rest of the ingredients.
Put on the slow cookers lid and cook for 5 hours on low heat.
Once done, garnish as desired
Serve warm.
Nutrition:
Calories 197
Total Fat 4 g
Saturated Fat 0.5 g
Cholesterol 135 mg
Sodium 790 mg
Total Carbs 31 g

Fiber 12.2 g
Sugar 2.5 g
Protein 11 g

Beanless Garden Soup

Preparation Time: 10 minutes
Cooking Time: 4 hrs. 5 minutes

Servings: 04
Ingredients:
1 medium onion, diced
2 cloves garlic, minced
1 green bell pepper, diced
1 red bell pepper, diced
2 carrots, peeled and diced
1 medium zucchini, diced
1 small eggplant, diced
1 hot banana pepper, seeded and minced
1 jalapeño pepper, seeded and minced
1 can (28 ounce) diced tomatoes
3 cups vegetable broth
1½ tablespoon chili powder
2 teaspoons smoked paprika
1 tablespoon cumin
2 tablespoons fresh oregano, chopped
2 tablespoons fresh cilantro, chopped
Salt and black pepper to taste
A few dashes of liquid smoke
Directions:
In a slow cooker, add olive oil and onion.
Sauté for 5 minutes then toss in the rest of the ingredients.
Put on the slow cookers lid and cook for 4 hours on low heat.

Once done mix well.
Serve warm.
Nutrition:
Calories 305
Total Fat 11.8 g
Saturated Fat 2.2 g
Cholesterol 56 mg
Sodium 321 mg
Total Carbs 34.6 g
Fibers 0.4 g
Sugar 2 g
Protein 7 g

Black-eyed Pea Soup with Olive Pesto

Preparation Time: 10 minutes
Cooking Time: 3 hrs. 5 minutes

Servings: 04
Ingredients:
Soup:
1 leek, trimmed
1 tablespoon olive oil
1 clove garlic, chopped
1 small carrot, chopped
1 stem fresh thyme, chopped
1 (15 ounce) can black-eyed peas, drained and rinsed
2½ cups vegetable broth
½ teaspoon salt
¼ teaspoon black pepper
Pesto:
1¼ cups pitted green olives

¼ cup parsley leaves
1 clove garlic
1 teaspoon capers, drained
1 tablespoon olive oil
Directions:
In a slow cooker, add olive oil, carrot, leek, and garlic.
Sauté for 5 minutes then toss in the rest of the soup ingredients.
Put on the slow cookers lid and cook for 3 hours on low heat.
Meanwhile, blend the pesto ingredients in a blender until smooth.
Blend the soup in the slow cooker with a hand mixer.
Top with prepared pesto.
Serve warm.
Nutrition:
Calories 72
Total Fat 15.4 g
Saturated Fat 4.2 g
Cholesterol 168 mg
Sodium 203 mg
Total Carbs 28.5 g
Sugar 1.1 g
Fiber 4 g
Protein 7.9 g

Spinach Soup with Basil

Preparation Time: 10 minutes
Cooking Time: 5hrs. 5 minutes

Servings: 06
Ingredients:
8 ounces potatoes, diced
1 medium onion, chopped

1 large clove of garlic, chopped
1 teaspoon powdered mustard
3 cups water
¼ teaspoon salt
Ground cayenne pepper
½ cup packed fresh dill
10 ounces frozen spinach
Directions:
In a low cooker, add olive oil and onion.
Sauté for 5 minutes then toss in rest of the soup ingredients.
Put on the slow cookers lid and cook for 5 hours on low heat.
Once done, puree the soup with a hand blender.
Serve warm.
Nutrition:
Calories 162
Total Fat 4 g
Saturated Fat 1.9 g
Cholesterol 25 mg
Sodium 101 mg
Total Carbs 17.8 g
Sugar 2.1 g
Fiber 6 g
Protein 4 g

Red Lentil Salsa Soup

Preparation Time: 10 minutes
Cooking Time: 17 minutes
Preparation Time: 27 minutes
Servings: 06
Ingredients:
1¼ cups red lentils, rinsed

4 cups of water
½ cup diced red bell pepper
1¼ cups red salsa
1 tablespoon chili powder
1 tablespoon dried oregano
1 teaspoon smoked paprika
¼ teaspoon black pepper
¾ cup frozen sweet corn
Salt to taste
2 tablespoons lime juice

Directions:

In a saucepan, add all the ingredients except the corn.
Put on saucepans lid and cook for 15 minutes at a simmer.
Stir in corn and cook for another 2 minutes.
Serve.

Nutrition:
Calories 119
Total Fat 14 g
Saturated Fat 2 g
Cholesterol 65 mg
Sodium 269 mg
Total Carbs 19 g
Fiber 4 g
Sugar 6 g
Protein 5g

Caldo Verde a la Mushrooms

Preparation Time: 10 minutes
Cooking Time: 5 hrs. 5 minutes

Servings: 08

Ingredients:
- ¼ cup olive oil
- 10 ounces button mushrooms, cleaned, and sliced
- 1½ teaspoons smoked paprika
- 1 pinch ground cayenne pepper
- 1 teaspoon salt
- 1 large onion, diced
- 2 cloves garlic, minced
- 2 pounds russet potatoes, peeled and diced
- 7 cups vegetable broth
- 8 ounces kale, sliced
- ½ teaspoon black pepper

Directions:

In a pan, heat cooking oil and sauté mushrooms for 12 minutes.

Season the mushrooms with salt, cayenne pepper, and paprika.

Add olive oil and onion to a slow cooker.

Sauté for 5 minutes then toss in rest of the soup ingredients.

Put on the slow cookers lid and cook for 5 hours on low heat.

Once done, puree the soup with a hand blender.

Stir in sautéed mushrooms.

Serve.

Nutrition:
- Calories 231
- Total Fat 20.1 g
- Saturated Fat 2.4 g
- Cholesterol 110 mg
- Sodium 941 mg
- Total Carbs 20.1 g
- Fiber 0.9 g
- Sugar 1.4 g
- Protein 4.6 g

Shiitake Mushroom Split Pea Soup

Preparation Time: 10 minutes
Cooking Time: 6 hours
Preparation Time: 6 hours 10 minutes
Servings: 12
Ingredients:
 1 cup dried, green split peas
 2 cups celery, chopped
 2 cups sliced carrots
 1½ cups cauliflower, chopped
 2 ounces dried shiitake mushrooms, chopped
 9 ounces frozen artichoke hearts
 11 cups water
 1 teaspoon garlic powder
 1½ teaspoon onion powder
 ½ teaspoon black pepper
 1 tablespoon parsley
 ½ teaspoon ginger
 ½ teaspoon ground mustard seed
 ½ tablespoon brown rice vinegar
Directions:
Add all the ingredients to a slow cooker.
Put on the slow cookers lid and cook for 6 hours on low heat.
Once done, garnish as desired.
Serve warm.
Nutrition:
Calories 361
Total Fat 16.3 g
Saturated Fat 4.9 g
Cholesterol 114 mg
Sodium 515 mg
Total Carbs 29.3 g

Fiber 0.1 g
Sugar 18.2 g
Protein 3.3 g

Velvety Vegetable Soup

Preparation Time: 10 minutes
Cooking Time: 2hrs 2 minutes

Servings: 4
Ingredients:
½ sweet onion, chopped
4 garlic cloves, chopped
1 small head broccoli, chopped
2 stalks celery, chopped
1 cup green peas
3 green onions, chopped
2¾ cups vegetable broth
4 cups leafy greens
1 (15 ounce) can of cannellini beans
Juice from 1 lemon
2 tablespoons fresh dill, chopped
5 fresh mint leaves
1 teaspoon salt
½ cup coconut milk
Fresh herbs and peas, to garnish
Directions:
In a slow cooker, add olive oil and onion.
Sauté for 2 minutes then toss in the rest of the soup ingredients.
Put on the slow cookers lid and cook for 2 hours on low heat.
Once done, blend the soup with a hand blender.
Garnish with fresh herbs and peas.
Serve warm.
Nutrition:

Calories 205
Total Fat 22.7 g
Saturated Fat 6.1 g
Cholesterol 4 mg
Sodium 227 mg
Total Carbs 26.1 g
Fiber 1.4 g
Sugar 0.9 g
Protein 5.2 g

Sweet Potato and Peanut Soup

Preparation Time: 10 minutes
Cooking Time: 4 hrs. 5 minutes

Servings: 06
Ingredients:
1 tablespoon water
6 cups sweet potatoes, peeled and chopped
2 cups onions, chopped
1 cup celery, chopped
4 large cloves garlic, chopped
1 teaspoon salt
2 teaspoons cumin seeds
3½ teaspoons ground coriander
1 teaspoon paprika
½ teaspoon crushed red pepper flakes
2 cups vegetable stock
3 cups water
4 tablespoons fresh ginger, grated
2 tablespoons natural peanut butter
2 cups cooked chickpeas
4 tablespoons lime juice

Fresh cilantro, chopped
Chopped peanuts, to garnish

Directions:

In a slow cooker, add olive oil and onion.
Sauté for 5 minutes then toss in the rest of the soup ingredients except chickpeas.
Put on the slow cookers lid and cook for 4 hours on low heat.
Once done, blend the soup with a hand blender.
Stir in chickpeas and garnish with cilantro and peanuts.
Serve warm.

Nutrition:

Calories 201
Total Fat 8.9 g
Saturated Fat 4.5 g
Cholesterol 57 mg
Sodium 340 mg
Total Carbs 24.7 g
Fiber 1.2 g
Sugar 1.3 g
Protein 15.3 g

Conclusion

Those who follow a plant-based diet may need a little more carefully to prepare their meals. It can make all the difference to equip yourself with some dietary knowledge. Read our guides on vegetarian protein sources, where you can get vitamin B12 as well as the best plant sources of omega-3, may be useful.

When you change your diet drastically, starting gradually may be beneficial–maybe adding two or three meals based on plants, or days, a week. It helps the body to adapt to new foods and shifts in the percentage of certain nutrients, such as fiber. It also allows you to experiment with new foods over a period of time and create some store cupboard staples.

Weight loss is an almost certain result you will enjoy once you start the plant-based diet, but this is not the only benefit that you will enjoy. Think of all those activities you have always wanted to pursue but shelved because you simply had no energy left after your usual days work.

Well, time to dust off those hobbies and the things you enjoy doing, because on the plant-based, you will have more energy for your daily work and play!

Something that many learn is that a diet is almost only as good as the number of recipes it has in its repertoire. The benefits of a particular diet may be numerous, but if you are forced to have the same stuff every breakfast, lunch and dinner, even the most avid supporter of the lot would probably have problems sustaining the diet. This is where I am most happy to say that the plant-based diet has quite some leeway for the concoction of various different recipes, and it is the purpose of this book to bring you some of the more delicious and easy-to-prepare meals for your gastronomic pleasure!

For the beginners as well as the adepts, the recipes contained within are created specifically to be appealing to your palate while not requiring you to literally spend the whole day in the kitchen! Concise and to the point, the recipes break down meal preparation requirements in a simple step by step format, easy for anyone to understand.

Dont forget to exercise. It has always been said that dieting is an effective way to lose weight. However, to keep the weight off, exercise is required. Many studies have shown that exercising while dieting is actually the best way to lose weight. Firstly, the diet becomes more effective and you lose weight faster if you exercise. But it also gets you in the habit of continuing your exercise when your diet is complete.

www.ingramcontent.com/pod-product-compliance
Lightning Source LLC
Chambersburg PA
CBHW071443070526
44578CB00001B/205